Preface

How do we re-enter our world after over a year of lockdown? Is it safe to come out of our caves?

The pandemic and many other unprecedented trials these past year have caused some of us to be crises mode or stewing in anxiety. For those who have suffered from abuse, have PTSD or emotional trauma, this last year may have amplified the anxiety, fear and sense of powerlessness. For others it's hard to talk about because we can't see the wounds and don't have the words, we just know there's a good reason to be afraid—look at all the proof the last year has shown us!

i

Enclosed in this book are powerful tools to bring forth your dreams. I've taught these tools in my classes and coaching, and they work. Spiritual Power Tools are transformative and teach you that every situation in your life can actually become a vehicle for your success.

Personal fulfillment, or success is not the outcome of strenuous work, strict planning or relentless ambition, but rather of understanding ourselves as spirits in bodies. When we are bathed or marinated in spiritual principles from the inside out, utilizing spiritual law is easy!

You will learn spiritual power tools that can easily be applied to create success in your life. Spiritual power tools are tools which use spiritual laws in the natural world. We are actively using pure spiritual laws and principles, or 'spiritual tools', for natural and effortless fulfillment of your dreams. An example of a tool is when we truly have and experience the inner qualities of success: ease, feeling healthy, fulfilled, connected to and serving people who matter to us, meaningfulness, love, peace, inner strength—when we experience these qualities and live in these qualities, we attract everything that matches those qualities. That is success on a very personal level!

There are two levels of creation, the natural and the spiritual. In the natural side is duality: giving is losing. If you give someone a slice of your pie, you have less. Competition means there is a winner and a loser, and limits decide how you will live. Limits of money, energy, health, career or social standing, obligations, morals, standards…. all set what is possible, or define your purpose. There is always something outside you, controlling you. The joys of life are fleeting because the goal posts are

SPIRITUAL POWER TOOLS FOR SUCCESS

Dream Fulfillment Toolkit

Brooke Scudder Andrews

Published by UTOPIA PRESS

DEDICATION

This book is for Rob, the love of my life.

always just outside your grasp. If only ____ would happen, then I'd be successful and happy. I need this… I need that.

Spiritual law is the opposite of natural law in some ways and limitless in other ways. For example, in Spiritual law, when you give, you receive—forgiveness or love, is is shared and increased. The giver and the receiver both have more. Peace is one of the many signs of being inside Spiritual law, another one is, teaching is learning. What we share in knowledge, we increase in ourselves. In this book we are learning about and using spiritual power tools for success.

The spiritual side, or subtle energy, impulses or seed ideas from the super conscious are always first in creation- these actually create the physical. As you use and practice the Spiritual Power Tools, you begin to attract all the things, people, situations that bring you that same feeling or inner sense of love, ease, success, dream fulfillment. You may also attract situations that help you develop or choose these qualities. These good things come from every level from which you can receive.

When we are are spiritually aligned with the universe— it begins to create for us, and in alignment with the God of our heart. We experience success and fulfillment of our dreams because of the deep personal nature of our creativity being in alignment with our larger Soul purpose. When you are doing your Soul purpose on earth, there is deep satisfaction even though it might be difficult or challenging. You are doing what you came to do. You were born for a reason and on purpose! You actually have a soul mission for this life, when you do it, you experience success and deep fulfillment.

HEAVEN IS A PRACTICE NOT A DESTINATION

Except the LORD build the house,
they labor in vain that build it.

Psalm 127

"WE GLORY IN TRIBULATIONS." ROM 5:3

Spiritual Power Tools for Success

1.TOOL NUMBER ONE, TURN TO LOVE

Close your eyes, fall in love. Stay there. ~ Rumi

Turn away from the problem or what you think you need and turn to Good. Turn away from lack, the crises, bad mood, anxiety, fear, sense of doom, and turn straight to good. Turn away from what you think you want to create and Turn to Love, to Universal Source, to Grace whatever you call it.. The soul responds to willingness, so even if you feel you aren't doing this right, have a willingness to look towards Love. Whatever your name for the Supreme Being is, Universe, Life, Source, Mother Father God, God, Jesus, Krishna, Buddha, just turn towards this good. That is the first power tool and it should fill you with a sense of awe. There is no other rule for this first power tool. Turn to God and rest. Sense what this feels like. Sense the living intelligence in all beings. Say gently to yourself, I am one with God and Her Love surrounds me now. Say this until you sense it, and any time you want to.

2.PRAISE

God's work is finished now and must manifest.

—Florence Scovel Shinn

Take a moment to relax and close your eyes. Yield utterly to Source. Just allow all limits to disappear into the nothingness from which they came. Release limits. Take a few minutes to surrender. Hear your breath. With your inner Eye, **look up.** Notice your 7th Chakra on top of your head. Notice what's up there. Allow yourself to KNOW. Allow yourself in this moment to know something the Greater part of yourself wants you to know.

Your higher Self "messages" will have a tone of, 'something wonderful is about to happen'. Good news is coming! Dive into this Idea for a moment. Just feel what it feels like. Something wonderful is about to happen. Good news!!! Your Higher Self might add onto this feeling, but realize you are inviting a communication with ALL THAT IS. You don't need to know what that is. Just the giddiness… the wakeful rest, the letting go of trying to make things happen. Something wonderful is about to happen! Good news, a good call, a letter, a surprise that is beyond wonderful. Sense this… GOOD NEWS!!!

Raise your arms in a V and say YESSS! Celebrate in advance. Something wonderful is about to happen! Jump up and bounce around full of uncontainable joy. Shout Yesssssss!

You are about to get a ping from the universe. Today

Wonderful will demonstrate and you will know. You are that powerful! Stand in your mind with power with your Wonder Woman stance and shout in your soul. YESSS! Feel what wakes up. Sense your Yes Self. Create your YES self. Sense what inner body awakens and comes radiantly alive when you are in your Power Yes. This is with whom we are working in this book.

If you get a sense that she doesn't exist, then make her up. Create her. Wake her up! Wake up! Arise! Your Divine Self is here, in her glory and perfection!

Imagine yourself as a goddess! She will show up in your mind in full form and you will know that your belief just opened the door for her to come into your awareness. She exists to the degree that you are conscious of her, and that doesn't mean she doesn't exist if you are not aware of her—you are part of her. She is part of you. She is your Higher Self.

She is sexless, so might appear as a sun, light, a deity. See yourself in a mighty position, see yourself in your minds eye not as the Force is with you, but YOU ARE THE FORCE. Sense an inner feeling as you do this. What shifts or becomes radiant?

When I do this it's a very soft, bowed head and a knowing happy heart. It takes no effort on your part. None at all. You are just the shell the Universe flows through. You are the lens which you can open or close: Truth, Love. Health. Courage, Life flows, light as a feather, but with the unstoppable power to insist on Truth.

See yourself as an unstoppable superhero, or as a goddess. But one you do not mess with. By this I don't mean an ego based superhero, but as one with the force to insist on bold health, insist on love, insist on mercy. To not be shaken by anything or anyone. Lord awaken my power to insist.

You assign something, which is nameless, a name. This is something that is beyond time and space and words, but it has a distinct feeling tone, it is the feeling of Something Wonderful is About to Happen, YESSS! It is radiance; it is light that is brighter than other light, like sun on snow, or sunlight reflecting on a still lake. Or not light. It is knowledge and understanding and good all at once. Assign a name, color, light, tone or feeling tone to this, so you know when you're in it and when you're not. Your YES Self is not your circumstances, facts, all the reasons why you can't do something. There are natural laws of earth and spiritual laws- you either are in one zone or the other. We are introducing the concept that you are both a spirit and a body. This concepts allows your spiritual self to pierce your natural life and demonstrate what it can do. Your spirit self and your body self each has its differing set of laws as real as gravity, and as real as eternity. Throughout the day, allow this idea, "Something wonderful is going to happen today. Today is a wonderful day, because something wonderful is going to happen." You may want to get a marker and write that out on your mirror, make a sticky note. Remind yourself. Note what happens, or how this shows up.

Matthew 5:14

"You are the light of the world. A town built on a hill cannot be hidden. Nor do people light a lamp and hide it under a bowl (or behind karma). Instead they put their light on its stand, where it gives light to everyone in the house. In the same way, let your light shine before others, that they may see your good deeds and glorify your Father in heaven.

This means that if you don't use your gifts, such as your ability to use light (or wholeheartedly declaring extremely wonderful news—which is spiritual understanding- the holy spirit within you), you will lose consciousness that you have these gifts. Use them. The first idea, abundance is possible, and the second idea, something wonderful is going to happen, are simple and powerful.

When you get very happy and a make a declaration you imprint the universe. Just don't be specific- allow it to show you how close It Knows the hidden secrets of your heart.

Ephesians 3:20-21
Now to Him who is able to do exceedingly abundantly above all that we ask or think, according to the power that works in us.

Spiritual Power Tools

1. Turn to God.

2. Praise

3.SPRITUAL VISION

The resurrection is the death of the belief that we are separate from God. – Ernest Holmes, The Science of Mind.

The Very Best Case Scenario Visioning or VBCS is easy, once you get the hang of it. You are asking the One who Created your Spirit what is your plan for my life in a specific area. You must assume a posture of extreme humility to allow this spiritual wisdom to animate your awareness. Here's the short version:

A. Humbly Ask God What is My Very Best Case Scenario in ____ area? (personal, work, career, love, things, situations, relationships... you name it. You are asking for aspects of His Plan for your life)

B. What Must I become to embody this? (energetically, emotionally, spiritually)

C. What must I release?

D. What Gifts skill and talents to I already have to create this?

E. Say Yes.

Here is the long version. It's good to practice the long version until you have a sense of how this works.

This is where your prayer chair and your meditation come in handy. You may have a sense of what you want guidance on. Have this in your mind. Soften. Feel the inside of your head as if it were a lake and it is smoothing any waves. Just relax and let go and allow your heart to expand and relax. You may want to sense your heart beat, your breathing. Allow your intellect to let go of what you want to happen here. The *intellect will never understand this* and will *actively rebel* so you must turn your intellect off and **turn your heart on.** The intellect or analyzer is a very small part of your brain and awareness and **you are allowing the whole you to participate** not just the analyzer.

In your prayer chair, surrender what you think ought to happen. Sense the Divine already in you. **Be very still and quiet your mind. You want to spend a few minutes to really dial into the Holy Spirit, so aim for an inner presence of Christ, or a divine presence in your heart. Soften and be gracious.**

Allow God's Highest Vision for this situation to come to you.

Allow the God of Your Heart to communicate with you. So be very quiet and still.

You have a unique intuitional system that is only activated by surrendering to what is. You have a unique relationship to the God of Your Heart, by your religious upbringing and experience, and my words might throw you off. Use your own intuition and inner knowing. Some people hear, some people see, some people know, or feel. One thing is that the first thing that will pop up is the monkey mind. You will begin to know the difference between your monkey mind that is always chattering nonsense and TRUTH.

It will flash, or linger, the only way I know it's from the Divine is that it is always inspiring and uplifting, and often an idea I never thought of. The Divine must be invoked, as we have free will, it will not come unless you invoke it and are quiet inside enough to hear, see or know or sense. Even sensing that you've done your best is enough to start the process – you don't have to see or know a thing, you just start inviting, and going through the steps.

Later on, a sentence in a book, or words of a song, or a conversation you overheard, with stand out so strongly, you will know something in that conversation is meant for you. The Divine speaks in a language that will not frighten you, so it may come though a dog giving you the look of grace when you've touched on the right plan, or a bird will start singing a beautiful song. You will know. It may be the sky is particularly beautiful, or the light in someone's face. You already have a relationship with the Divine; this process will bring it forward in your life. This image from your Higher Self will flash by your mind. You may want to write what you can in your journal, or have scratch paper to jot any idea or image or words that come from the still small place. Sooner or later with practice, It will come. It will seem too good to be true, or have peace or a feeling tone. Record it even if it is a sense of a fur, or softness. Or a tune, or a sound, or a sentence in a loving voice. Or all of this or none of it. You have your way. Begin even if nothing happens. Know that you have indeed created with God even if you don't notice a thing. You have! It is a new language that you learn new word by new word. These words, images, flashes are **the living waters of life.**

Begin..

Breathe slowly and deeply to consciously slow down.

Feel into an awareness of Love's Presence in this moment.

Be quiet, still and listen with sacred reverence. Sense a feeling tone, you might imagine a rose and notice the qualities of the rose. Aim towards the Divine. Just be open and know and rest in LOVES PRESENCE.

You will know the VBCS visions from the Divine by their joy and a certain quality of light that is unlike other visions.

The monkey mind can make visions as well, as well as your family, friends who mean well, spouse, church, community, friends. They can mean well, but if you are in someone else's vision it comes with limits and, it is probably not God's vision which is all powerful. Here we are going to Gods Highest Vision for you. There is said in the bible, have no Gods before God. Here, in this process, you are not allowing any person, place, thing to have more importance than the Highest Holiest Wisdom.

If, in this process, you feel apathy, you can be certain you are not in harmony with your highest vision, which is always life giving. No one can do this for you. This is between you and your Highest Self.

Allow society's visions to vanish.

Allow anyone's vision for you to vanish

Allow old past life patterns to vanish like mist.

Be so quiet on the inside and crane your ear as if the greatest secret in the Universe was about to whispered in your ear.

Jesus is always whispering some great thing to us, Always!

So, this practice of VBCS is a great way to tune into the higher dimensions that are always guiding us- and that would be our highest goal and outcome. To have clear guidance on what is yours to do in this life, so when you die you have the greatest sense of accomplishment, and know that you did make a difference. The funny thing is that you couldn't die, even if you wanted to. You might sleep, but VBCS Visioning wakes up the eternal you and puts it at the center of your being. You become not only really powerful, your goals change and being happy, or joyful or peaceful becomes really important, as that is the vibration or channel you receive on. Power takes on a new meaning. God can't really work with people who choose to be grumpy all the time. You choose Gods vision because you might be tired of being grumpy all the time, and sense there is a better way of doing things and you are open to learning. That is how the Course in Miracles was written. The transcriber worked in a very competitive university, where everyone was destroying everyone else just to keep their job. Helen said, there's got to be another way. This is funny because she was an atheist, and a strict non-believer, yet she was the person who brought about the Course in Miracles. Here is the top trained university scholar saying, after being an expert, that all of her learning is not serving her. This is where we need to be if we are going to ask spirit for an answer, we have to be clear, we are going to listen to the Divine. Otherwise, there's really no point.

Real humility before God is letting go of every Spiritual teacher you ever had, every problem you ever had, and not having any gods before God. It is letting go of what you think Spirituality and Religion is. It is releasing right and wrong, tit for tat, karma, revenge, payback, what is due, what you think you are entitled to. It is letting go of why you think you need to be sick, or someone else's problem. It is letting go of who you think you are, and what others call you, your titles and honors, your wicked secrets you keep hidden even to yourself. The sins of others. Your agendas – every one of them. You gotta let everything go so **Truth can rewrite your concept of self.**

When you have surrendered, and open for God, you have a silent place where something wonderful is about to be known, but you don't know what that is. You can't put into words or useful images or sounds Gods holy name for you, but the part of you that lives in God and your mind now has a channel.

There are really no words for that which is beyond our greatest expectation. The unlimited can not be put into words. If you hear a word, it is a symbol for something that cannot be contained in a word.

Ask, What must I release?

What I mean to say is you are ready and willing for something great to come into your life. This willingness might be for bliss and love, real love of your self, and seeing how exquisite you really are. This will change you forever. God's Highest Vision for your must be beckoned by releasing what you created so God can create through you.

Denial can be really useful sometimes. Declare, and intend, or simply postulate anything not the Highest and True for you to be unreal and non-existent. Allow anything that needs to go, to go with grace. Something has to go so something new can come, if only an idea of it's not possible to be in the Kingdom of God. Ideas may come up and you are to mentally vanish those ideas, see mist disappearing. See images fall into dust. You may see a person, see them walk away or vanish. Allow anything not in alignment to go. You might imagine a golden angelic broom sweeping clean your path. You don't record this because it is already gone.

Ask, What gifts, skills and talents do I already have?

What do I already have that is in alignment with my Very Best Case Scenario? Just allow yourself to become aware of what you already have that will help you in creating and executing God's Highest Vision, His Very Best Case Scenario for you. As a creation of the Divine, which you are, You already have the whole kingdom. What in your past has prepared you for this? Destiny is about what your life, your learning, has prepared you for. Allow something unusual, something unknown to be presented, which is still who you are as a creation of the Divine, so be still and quiet and allow.

There may be an awareness of you being the question and the solution as well as a wise loving onlooker. This will always have a tone of extremely good news, inspiration or motivation.

Ask.. is there anything else?

For some people this is where all the information comes, for others they are met with silence. Be still and allow God to give you the energetic supply to fulfill your mission.

Give THANKS

If you saw, KNEW, or heard something it is already created. **Giving sincere Thanks allows more to come.** You want more to come, and to have an intuitional guidance check in, so being grateful for Divine Communication is like activating a pump. It is the on faucet. Lean into your gratitude that you had a space to meditate, and that your VBCS is already created and will come into being in the perfect way under grace and nothing can destroy or delay it. Faith without works doesn't exist, so know you will be doing things in a new way, have a new schedule, new relationships, people will leave your life, new ones will come in grace.

Good job! **You just wrote on the walls of eternity your essential truth.** You just created a divine blueprint in the universe.

You will move in the world in a new way as your Higher Self will not only be holding your hand, but clearing your way and giving you strength when you check in and ask for strength, or help, or a gracious new path. You will no longer go alone. Be grateful for this.

Rest in this awareness and receive light, allow your cup to overflow with love and bask in God's joy. Meditating after visioning is wonderful! And it's free! Some would say this is gravy, but this awareness is what animates your highest life. Now the Force is animating your life.

You already have the essence of what you are seeking.

Celebrate! Allow any ideas or images, however they come to you, even words, to show you that not only is what God is asking is possible, but you are meant to develop and grow into the strength, joy and life that you already have. This is like seeing a loving aspect of yourself that is about to become known to you. Draw or write in your journal.

Celebrate that you already have what is alignment with God's plan or Highest Vision. Become aware that you already have the whole kingdom because you are a holy child of God. Sense Deep Gratitude. Giving sincere Thanks creates a relationship for intuitive guidance throughout the day.

If you are not having spiritual vision and really want to know more about it, read A Course in Miracles from cover to cover a few times. The books about the Course in Miracles are not the Course in Miracles, which is hard to read and for that reason most people don't take the time and energy to read it. If you read it slowly, the words will actually reveal another meaning, right above the text.

You have your own way and it isn't mine. This may not be your cup of tea, however, The Course in Miracles awakens your Spiritual Vision which it actually calls the Holy Spirit. Many other spiritual texts refer to the Spiritual Eye in the same way.

To learn more about this method of Visioning, read Life

Visioning, by Michael Bernard Beckwith.

Spiritual Power Tools Covered.

1. Turn to God

2. Praise.

3. Spiritual Visioning: Despite my limited closed ideas, My Divine Self is actively showing me a wonderful thing (world of Spirit) that will happen (in the world of form).

4. TRANSFORMATION

Choose this day whom you will serve. – Joshua 24:15

Transformation is turning a problem into a solution using

Affirmative prayer

> Wikipedia says, "Affirmative prayer is a form of prayer or a metaphysical **technique that is focused on a positive outcome rather than a negative situation.** For example, a person who is experiencing some form of illness would focus the prayer on the desired state of perfect health and affirm this desired intention "as if already happened" rather than identifying the illness and then asking God for help to eliminate it."

Here is an example of Affirmative Prayer

There is that in you, Spirit, which is unconditioned regardless of what you have done to condition yourself. -Raymond Charles Barker

God-Mind is My Only Authority

God-Mind is my only authority. Today, I choose to focus on the Truth. Regardless of appearances, facts, situations, or challenges, there is only Once Sacred Truth about life. The Truth is that there is only God-Mind. I am made in the image of this Infinite One, and my use of God-Mind is the channel through which the Infinite reveals Itself.

Though conditions may appear as problems, lacks, and limitations, I choose to rise above those appearances and tune into a greater idea of Sacred Truth. I face facts squarely and with confidence. I now choose not to give any creative energy to negative facts or conditions. My energy, my focus, and my love is given to the creation of solutions, answers and the ideas of spiritual awareness for my life's enrichment.

There is that within me that knows and responds to the Truth of my being. I now call it forth and allow spiritual wholeness and intuitive revelation to flow by means of me with a sense of easy awareness. I love from Spirit power with peace, poise and confidence.

With joy and conviction, I give thanks as I release my word to the Infinite Law of Mind that knows what to do and how to do it to bring my word into from and experience. I am the authority of God in action as my life.

Prayer by Dr. Arleen Bump for Creative Thought Magazine

The five of Affirmative Prayer steps are:
1. Recognition (God Is)
2. Unification (I am in and of God and I feel this.)
3. Realization (Speaking into reality your desired good for example: say the *opposite of your problem* as if it's accomplished and you feel it done and good and know it works.)
4. Thanksgiving (Grateful Acceptance) and
5. Release (Letting go, let God)

By writing your own Affirmative Prayer you make it

yours. The main thing is to **feel into every one of the five steps.** It is not the words that you use that make the prayer powerful, it is **the feeling tone behind the words.**

If you examine the dynamics of the Lord's Prayer, you will see that affirmative prayer uses the Lord's Prayer as a template in some ways. What someone is looking for is what they find.

Affirmative Prayer how to from a Center for Spiritual Living Class:
A treatment should be done in a calm, expectant manner with deep, inner conviction of its reality-- without any fear that the human mind must make it effective. Man's life is rooted in the Universal and the Eternal, which is none other than the life of God. The healing process, so far as it may be termed process, is in becoming conscious of this eternal truth. **Treatment should always incorporate a conscious recognition that health has always been ours, abundance has always been ours, happiness and peace have always been ours: they are ours now, for they are the very essence and Truth of our being.**

Steps of Spiritual Mind Treatment
1.RECOGNITION
We begin with the recognition of God as the essence of all and the very ground of all being. This is the most important step, because you are turning consciously to the truth of Life. Do not proceed with your treatment until

you are fully steeped in this recognition. Speak the word of recognition that God is all.

2.UNIFICATION

All your emotions, body and intuition assist in the full recognition of yourself as Divine substance. *Know and feel the unity of all in God.* Declare this as True. I am now thinking with the Mind of God.

3.REALIZATION

Turn completely away from the issue at hand and affirm God manifesting its perfect qualities as your life. ***Catch inspiration and thrill in this Divine realization.*** See it, feel it, in every detail. Open up all avenues of thought and let Reality through. Remember that you area finding and realizing this truth for yourself and that this treatment takes place within your own mind. That is all that is needed for the healing to occur. As you align your own consciousness and declare that all good is already yours by your very nature, the Power of God reveals It's presence in all things.

4. GRATITUDE

Open your heart with gratitude for this Blessing occurring in your life now.

5. RELEASE

Let go. There is no more for you to do. The law is neutral and always works. Know that it is done now.

Secrets of Effective Treatment
* Remember to listen. Although you are praying for a specific purpose, you are also aligning yourself with Infinite wisdom.

* Go Slowly and follow any inner guidance that directs your words and ideas into complete alignment with the Divine.
* Speak the word of your heart. Your own truth cannot be denied.
* Emphasize the inner qualities and leave the outer manifestation to God.
* Be passionate. Pray with Intense joy. Miracles are at hand.
* Its is all so amazingly good!

To learn more about Affirmative Prayer, take a foundations class at your local Center for Spiritual Living.

Spiritual Power Tools so far..

1. Turn to God.

2. Raise your energy: Something wonderful *will* happen through me.

3. Spiritual Visioning: Despite my limited closed ideas, My Divine Self is actively showing me a wonderful thing (world of Spirit) that will happen (in the world of form).

4. Transformation.

5. GRATITUDE

It is the spirit that quickeneth, the flesh profiteth
nothing. The words that I speak unto you, they are spirit, they
are life. —John 6:63

The Key is to write the letter as if you are already
enjoying your answered prayers. Write a **daily letter**
thanking God for all the Good in your life, and read it
aloud with passion for the best results. When you write
another side letter for another person, it activates the

Spiritual Power. As we give we receive. The side letter can be for a random person, someone in India, or someone close, or even an enemy (wishing them their highest good).

The rules:

1. Write out gratitude statements for **what you appreciate now.**

2. Write out gratitude statements for **what you want, as though you have already received it.**

3. Recognize, with gratitude that the **Universal law works on your behalf.** Your unification with God as partner opens the door to Universal power working on your behalf.

4. **Raise your energy before starting;** such as I am statements, gratitude or reading inspirational material. Feel into your desired good as if it were already in existence.

Dear _____(your word for God, such as Universal Love, Source, Truth, Omnipresence, Omnipotence, Omniscience…)

Thank you for my----- List <u>what you **have**</u> that you are grateful for. Thank you for my home, my loving relationships, my car, my sense of humor, my nature hikes, etc……

1. _____

2. _____

3. _____

4. _____

Thank you for my…… List <u>what you</u> **want** but don't have as gratitude statements **as though you already have them**

1._____

2._____

3._____

4. _____

Thank you God for your Universal Power operating in my life.

For all this good and more, I give great thanks.

I now release these words to the Law, truth and power of the universe and know that it is done.

With gratitude and love,

Your name_____

The added rule is that you must check in during the day and ask for guidance. Ask, am I on track? Is this the right thing and really get quiet and listen with your whole heart.

Just try it and learn to see that everything that ever happened is from a loving universe. You can ask it questions, say what is on your mind. Put it in an envelope and place in your holiest book. If you have no holy books then a poetry book, or you favorite book. It might be a picture book. Let the letter marinate for awhile and read a week or a day later. Notice what warms your heart.

Below is a letter that is based on Catherine Ponder, who says to say what is really in your heart.. don't ask for middling things, go all the way.

We are invoking spiritual Law when we write gratitude letters. You release the things you've given thanks for and trust the laws of the universe will do the work. You are turning your trust in Universal Love. You do nothing more than give thanks and check in to see if you are going in the right direction.

1. Write out a letter for what you appreciate now.

2. Write out gratitude for what you want, as though you've already received them.

3. Recognize with gratitude that the universal power can be used to receive all that you want.

4. God enables Universal power to work on your behalf. So, you are finding your partnership with Spirit to co-create with you. You already know that what you put your attention on increases, and you know that giving thanks puts you in the spiritual law. "…those who can have, can have more."

Here is an example of a letter. (Thank you to Catherine Ponder and May McCarthy for inspiration!)

Dear Highest God of our Most Loving Universe,

Omnipotence, Omniscience and Omnipresence is all in all, so It's in me and I am

turning and tuning into my internal loving Divine Vibration at One with God. As I do this I notice my breath. I am breathing in God. This feels like_____ . (happy peaceful yet poised and giddy, jumping for Joy!)

Thank you, Lord, for my life, my strength and my joy of being. Thank you that I am abundantly provided for as I follow my path. Thank you that your abundance includes that I slept well last night- thank you! Thank you that I am alive, full of joyful lifeforce and awake to you and your ways. Thank you for all your marvelous blessings!

Thank you for working in me, though me, by me and for me, to will and to do that which is mine to do. Thank you for showing me what to do, when to do it, how to do it in order to experience my highest good in all my affairs. I am so grateful that you are Love, peace, joy, ease, wisdom, and abundance. And, as you are these qualities and so much more, and you created me in your image and likeness, I am all these qualities! Your power created me to be the perfect expression of your creation here on earth. I accept this role and am delighted that my talents are being used in meaningful, satisfying, fulfilling, fun, easy, successful and abundant ways.

Thank you, Lord for my life. Everyone related to my life is blessed at all times and receives our good. Thank you that You and I attract interesting, marvelous people, family, partners, clients, neighbors, friends and community into my life, who are for my highest and best good. We enjoy each other's presence, talents and gifts. WE bless all others and we all experience success.

I love everyone and every one loves me. I love myself and am loved. I bless everyone and everyone blesses me. I bless myself and am blessed. I forgive everyone and everyone forgives me. I forgive myself and am forgiven. I am peace with poise and confidence. I am grateful for my physically fit, trim, toned, energetic, healthy body that is eternally youthful and increasingly more beautiful, whole and complete. Joy radiates in and though me to all our world. I am ease and live a charmed life. All that is mine to do is done easily and joyfully, and I experience my highest and best good at all times. I am wisdom and make right decisions as guided and directed by God. I am huge abundant prosperity with overflowing resources. Thank you so much!!!

Thank you Lord that I am rich beyond my wildest dreams with a minimum of _____ to use and enjoy, bless others with as God directs, and invest and increase. Thank you, Lord, that I am financially independent and free, and I am abundantly provided for as I follow my path.

*Thank you, Lord, for my spouse, who is my perfect loving mate. WE are so **blessed** and **happy** with YOU at the **center of our relationship**. Thank you God for my family, my friends, and my wonderful dog, and that **YOU are in the Center of all my relationships.** They are all such treasures to me. I live my purpose— I bless other and am blessed.*

*For all this good and so much more, I give great thanks and rest in Divine Love. I now release these words to Spiritual law and it is done better than I can imagine because **God doeth the works.** And so it is!*

Love,

To activate this Spiritual Power Tool in your life, **write a**

letter for someone else's success. Just write and affirmative testimony for either a random person, or someone you know and make it wonderful. You don't need to tell them about it. It's just that when we give success to others we receive it. To give is to receive, so be generous!

To learn more about Gratitude Prayers, read Path to Wealth, by May McCarthy

Very Best Case Scenario Steps so far…

1. Turn to **God.**

2. Something really wonderful *is in me* and acts through me. **Praise!**

3. **Vision**. Despite my limited closed ideas, My Divine Self is actively showing me a wonderful thing (world of Spirit) that will happen (in the world of form).

4. **Transformation.** I can actively transform problems (lower mind) into answers (Higher Mind) as I unite with the Universal Source as a co-creator.

5. Gratitude

6. WORKS

*The Word of God is the revelation to all the powers
and the possibilities of everyone's own being. Your
word is the power through which you make your belief
manifest. — Charles Fillmore*

I noticed a new dynamic when I returned to tennis a few
years ago, I was eager to play just like I did 20 years prior
with the United States Tennis Association or USTA. This
didn't happen—and—the more I put the pressure I placed
on myself, the worse I played.

During my first returning USTA matches, my nerves
overwhelmed me. I noticed the score, how great the
opponents played and sometimes I'd hear cheering for the
opponents and not us— which really sucked the wind
from my sails. I was focused on anything but the tennis
ball. The USTA matches made me extremely nervous
because my timing was off because I was focused on
something other than the game I was playing. In a court
of 2800 square feet and a 3 inch diameter ball with
unknown speed and direction, you need to have timing to

move in such a was as to meet the ball having the weight of your body moving into the ball, and your arm moving with force and at just the right height as to cancel the balls trajectory and force coming toward you and aim it in the other direction, so timing. Tennis requires inner stillness to even access this, and if your mind is all aflutter and anxious, you begin to play against yourself. I was older and less in shape and not tuned up, so the pressure I placed on myself was not realistic, but there you have it.

The tennis champions like Billie Jean King talk about the nerves, yet Billie turned it around and said, **Pressure is a Privilege.** One aspect of pressure is a privilege is that you only improve in tennis (or life) when you break *though* limits. Limits are exactly what holds you back. Think about that sentence, breaking through a limit. Limitless is of spirit and limit is of the natural world. In the action of breaking through perceived limits, on a subtle level, we reach into spirit for this breakthrough.

It's the same with muscle building. It's the repetition after you are feeling exhausted that actually increases the muscle. What gives you that push to continue after you are exhausted? What gives you idea that you can be stronger? The core of the idea? It's when we don't think we can do something and go for it, that we learn our limits, and that specific fear loosens its hold.

Frayed nerves are common to all athletes: you get all amped up the night before and can't sleep and are a bundle of nerves—some of those nerves are what gives you the edge—nerves means you care. Caring is beautiful, because it means that you've found your pot of gold. The things you deeply care about are where your joy is and your joy is your treasure. Joy is of God in you and its vibration can strengthen you to move mountains and overcome obstacles. ***Unless you are using the force against yourself.*** This idea goes into the heart of what is at stake with *The best or worst case scenario.* Extreme energy is there, but it's creating fear and not flow. Ernest Holmes says there is a force like electricity and it can be used for good or bad.

CHAOS

The idea of being in the middle of chaos and creation or fear and faith has deep roots that go back to 3000 BC and shows up in our current medical symbol as the caduceus—the rod with the snake wrapped around it. The snake staff in a nutshell is about the doctor being a link between sickness and health. Between life and death.

This ancient symbol of winged snake wrapped around a staff was first attributed to Thoth and Hermes, an ancient Egyptian/early Greek combined god known as far back as 16th century BC. This same god, known as Thrice Hermes was considered the modern Moses during the Renaissance. Moses, remember, had a staff that turned into a snake in the burning bush episode and after that it is referred to as the **staff of God.** The base image of our medical symbol is ancient! It carries the idea in the gestalt of our combined consciousness and is a distilled symbol that carries the idea of healing from thousands of years back of recorded time.

It's kind of funny that currently there is great fuss over where the snake and wings are placed on the staff – and that says which branch of medicine and don't confuse the nearly identical symbols. This is hilarious. The basic image has lived in our collective consciousness for thousands and thousands of years.

It is an idea said lightly touched on by Matthew in the bible: "Be ye therefore wise as serpents and harmless as doves". This is the Zone! Read on….

The significance of the serpent has been interpreted in many ways; sometimes the shedding of skin and renewal is emphasized as symbolizing rejuvenation, while other assessments center on the serpent as a symbol that unites and expresses the dual nature of the work of the physician, who deals with life and death, sickness and health. The ambiguity of the serpent as a symbol, and the contradictions it is thought to represent, reflect the ambiguity of the use of drugs, which can help or harm, as reflected in the meaning of the term *pharmakon*, which meant "drug", "medicine", and "poison" in ancient Greek.

I will come back to this staff, on with my tennis story..

The nerves before a tennis match are similar to hunting

dogs before the hunt. The dogs are wired and cocked and crying, full of pent up energy that will propel them on the chase. Some of those nerves mean you are all in! It feels like dynamite wants to go off and it can be used for you or against you. Some of it's adrenaline.

Victims use the force against themselves. I would tell myself before tennis with my frayed nerves..*I'm not a sporty person in general, old enough to be some of the opponent's grandmother, not an athletic build, not tall, not aggressive.* You name it. All my fears came up why I should lose. Victims are like that. Always blaming something.

My fears amplified with the adrenaline until I was a bibbering wreck. Just to blot out the mental chatter I began singing to myself, inspirational songs would come up. I sang loudly.. *but to myself.* I sang over the distractions, and tuned in to my game. This made me happier, but strangely, the more and intensely I sang (to myself), the better I played! Suddenly I played on a much higher level!

Singing, for me, was a bridge. Internal Singing directed my fear to joy so my energy that could work for me instead of against me. I had been in a choir the previous two years, so the songs that looped in my mind were inspirational.

When I turned to the songs within while I was waiting for the serve, I was more relaxed and I could focus on the tennis ball. My game changed to confident, sure-footed, energetic, I was having fun and was extremely accurate. When you are in this place you don't ask why, you run with it for as long as you can.

Whenever fear came up to paralyze me, I imagined I was singing with the choir *in harmony*, and maybe even the opponent was singing the harmonies. (Harmony is Health!) And it would shift my perspective, instead of the world being against me, the world was with me in an amazing way. I was filled with a certain joy—I played with joy, intensity, boldly and I didn't care whether there was a crowd rooting for my opponents or not. I instinctively knew to tune out everything and focus on the ball so intensely I could see the spin, the shadow, the curve, so my body instinctively knew where to run to be ahead of the ball. I had unending explosive power and felt as though I could play all day. This is the Zone!

At times it seemed as if time slowed so I could move ahead to the ball, and I knew where to run! When I played hard as I could, instead of feeling exhausted, my energy increased— I had more power than I knew what to do with. Somehow all that energy I was using against myself was grounded and usable as Bold and Accurate Power. Courage came out of nowhere. I was in a cosmic dance. There was no opponent- the net, the ball, the players, the ground, sky, birds all in a dance, all sending energy to each other. Every thing was alive, it seemed, and I was the energy of a dance with all that is.

In sports, this is called the Zone. The zone is that

special mental state where everything flows effortlessly and the player is playing at peak performance.

The Zone is very much like the Very Best Case Scenario visioning, can you see the similarities?

This is what tennis players say about the zone: The player in the zone does not perceive his opponent as a threat. Instead, the player perceives the opponent as a challenge and uses his skills to overcome this challenge. A tennis match becomes a problem-solving task and the player is focused only on finding the solutions.

The outcome hitting the ball in, winning a point, winning a match, reaching the finals- is not within your control. If you focus on the outcome, you will become anxious since deep inside you know that you cannot guarantee the result.

Being anxious only worsens your ability to play good tennis. That's why you need to focus on the process that is within your control direct all of your attention toward the ball and what you want to do with it. The process is your idea of how you want to send the ball away, which means that you IMAGINE the trajectory of the ball and where you want it to land. Keep your focus on the execution of the shot until it's finished.

The opposite of being decisive is being indecisive, which means that you don't have a clear goal. A player in the zone does not change his mind and does not doubt his decisions. Whatever decision comes to mind, he sticks with it, trusts it, and goes with it.

A player in the zone does not judge his shots as good or bad. He sees them only as feedback to indicate whether he needs to keep doing what's working or make slight adjustments. Judgment immediately triggers emotions, which break the flow and the zone state.

Another characteristic of being in the zone is having no sense of the past or future. The player is immersed in "the now". This allows him to use all of his brain capacity for solving the problem in the moment without distracting thoughts about the past and future.

This is the mental state, which produces super-human performances, amazing shots and winning streaks. **Any tennis player who is in this mental state is virtually unbeatable at their respective level of competition** - and at the elite level, you witness some unbelievable shot making.

A player who is in the zone experiences an unusual feeling of effortless power, allowing them to feel as if their racquet and body are powered by a turbo-charged engine, and they find their body gliding across the court and hitting with awesome power and minimum effort. **The strange part about this is - this powerful performance does not feel as if it is being controlled by the actual player!**

In fact, they'll often report feeling as if they weren't responsible for some of the amazing shots at all - as if their body was being guided and directed by a more powerful force (and this is exactly what is happening).

Almost every player at some stage in their career has experienced this feeling to some extent, and then wondered afterwards "how did I do that?"

This is the mystery that surrounds the zone - **why does it appear so fleetingly, and then disappear just as quickly as it came? And most of all - why can't we access it all the time?**

What is the powerful force which is guiding the body when you hit an unbelievable shot? The answer is the sleeping giant that resides inside all human beings - the subconscious mind, the source of all bodily movement which also stores all past tennis memories and experience.

When a player is 'zoning', their conscious mind becomes quiet (the normally busy, chattering mind we use all the time), and this allows their more powerful subconscious to run their performance on 'automatic pilot', in the way a computer runs software.

This allows their strokes to flow with effortless reflexes and power in a way that could never be matched by conscious thought.

This means that when you are in the zone, you have virtually no thought going through your mind

whatsoever, your body is just playing on automatic-pilot, powered directly by your subconscious mind.

This is not to say that your body is playing without instruction, on the contrary, it is simply getting its instructions from a more powerful and reliable source.

So how do we get into the zone? Everyone must find the method that best suits their needs, but one of the main ways is to **simply practice (in your daily training) thinking *absolutely nothing* while you are hitting!**

This prevents the weaker conscious mind from giving your body incorrect instructions, and allows your powerful subconscious (the sleeping giant within you, and control center of all bodily movement) to run your tennis on auto-pilot, as it is meant to.

WHAT CONTROLS THE ZONE?

I saw a video about a five-year-old boy who loved the piano. He played every chance that he got. He never had any formal lessons or training. In fact, some people told him he was too young and too small; but in spite of those comments, he continued practicing. The only song he really knew how to play was "Chopsticks." It's just a very simple tune.

One day, his father surprised him with tickets to the symphony to hear this world-renowned Italian pianist. They arrived early and the concert hall was just filling with people. On the way to their seats, the little boy noticed the beautiful grand piano up on the stage. When no one was watching, he snuck over, sat down and began to play his elementary version of "Chopsticks." The kid was playing chopsticks as the curtain began to rise. Everyone was expecting to see the world-renowned pianist. Instead, they saw this little five-year-old boy. He was so caught up in his world that he didn't realize what was happening. When he finally looked up, he was petrified.

Just as he was about to take off running toward his seat, he felt two big arms reaching around him from behind. It was the world-renowned pianist. He whispered in the little boy's ears, "Keep playing."

The little boy continued playing that elementary version of "Chopsticks." The world-renowned piano player started playing a Beethoven symphony piece that was scored in the same cadence and the same key. Under the direction of the master, he brought in the rest of the orchestra. First, the woodwinds, then the percussion, and then the brass.

The father sat there in the audience with tears. He never dreamed that simple tune that he had heard in his home so many times would no longer sound like "Chopsticks," but it would become a beautifully inspired, fully perfected,

Beethoven symphony. What happened? The master stepped in.

Sometimes in life, you may not feel like you have the talent, the strength or the ability, **but sometimes when you let go, the larger aspect of yourself comes in and works through you**. When you use what you have, **Universal Source will flow through you, and amazing things will begin to happen!**

"For it is God who works in you, both to will and to work for his good pleasure." Philippians 2:13

Where God or joy is there is courage. Singing for me is joy. So, an aspect of God is in Joy with me on the court when I sing to myself.

Can you identify what brings you joy? Unbreakable joy?

Coeur the root of Courage, means heart. Heart is of God. Love is an aspect of courage. Where God is there is no fear.

Singing songs of praise took me to a place I shared with the God of my Heart. Courage happened when I sang in my mind, joyful songs of praise. The mind cannot occupy fear and joy at the same time. Singing is a trick to get you into joy.. if that's your thing. Under pressure, increase your measure by turning to joy. One bit of God gave me wholeheartedness and that put me in the flow.

Now for you? Can you remember when you were at your best, when things came to you effortlessly? This is your map to your treasure. **Never forget those moments when God stepped in and how you arrived there. Or when you were in the Zone. This is what helps you next time.**

POWER MOMENTS

A power moment is a moment that changed your life for the better. A Distilled Power Moment is the moment recorded in a journal with other power moments.

What is a Power Moment? There are moments in your life when you were in utter awe. These moments where the impossible is better than you can imagine hold great power. It was great power that made them possible. In spirit, there is no time or space- when you mentally visit those places when your mountain was moved- you remember there is something beyond you that has your back.

Maybe the moment you received a huge sum of money that came out of nowhere, or the moment you received an honor that took your career on the fast track to success, the baby born moment, the I will marry you moment, the rain came when you needed it moments. The test you passed that made graduation possible. Someone was kind for no reason, just when you needed a hand. ..what ever happened —these moments have power. When we revisit them in our mind, we are reminded that it can happen again. When we say, something amazingly good happened in the past and it can happen again- and stay in faith, believing – even when we see nothing, we open the door to more good. Our consciousness is raised. It is our raised consciousness that does the works.

If you've ever had one moment of awareness of God making your way easier, or healing you or showing you love instead of fear, just one moment.. do you think God will withhold that from you again? Ever?

If you've ever been touched by spirit, it is there on purpose and it is with you forever. This awareness is eternal and you build on it every time you remember it. I say touched by spirit, the tennis language calls it the zone, which has lots of scientific documentation. Just watch Steph Curry or Roger Federer play and you will see what the zone looks like. Whatever you call it, we have these strong memories of being touched by God, so strongly, that if and when we do fall down again, we don't stay there—we have ammunition to get our fire back.

When we are in the pit, the dark night of the soul, the disaster that keeps getting worse, we might be having a pity party, and we might be screaming hallelujah in anxiety, hoping it will take hold, meanwhile we don't know to ask, "where is that list of really good things that happened?" And you won't be able to remember all those good moments because you will be in survival. That is the very reason why you **write the power moments down now!** And put the book in a place where you can add to it when good things happen. Keep it near and dear.

Raising up our fire when we don't think we can- in the middle of sickness, like remembering that we ourselves are a thermostat, not a thermometer, and suddenly we are reminded of who we really are—and decide to get strong and healthy, and let the outer take care of itself. The inner I telling Sickness- you will NOT defeat me. I have come back before and I will come back again. STRONGER! And then you have proof of all the times you did.

We need extra faith when we are in deep over our heads. **The power journal is faith distilled** like investment funds that keep growing with compounding interest. You must keep adding those moments and reliving the glory for the compounded distilled faith to see you through the inescapable trials of life.

It's what you do in the deep pit that determines your future. It can go either way. Your power journal helps you to create a brighter future, by being in your highest creative essence. It's not blind faith when you have a list of all the times extraordinary power stepped into your life. You have documented proof of your seen and unseen capabilities that made toast of the natural facts.

In the way, way, back olden times sheepherders had a rod to protect the sheep from predators and a staff or a shepherd's hook to keep the sheep in order. You can see some of these ancient staffs with cuneform in the British Museum and the Louvre. About two or three thousand years ago people in some areas wrote in cuneiform, which is easy to inscribe on a wooden stick. (It looks like chicken feet scratches) There was a practice of only marking miracles or amazing feats on the rods and staffs. There was limited space on the stick, so only the very best personal moments were recorded. After years or decades of miracle writing, the staff was covered accounts of extraordinary feats and unusual goodness, so even holding the staff could fill you with the power. And.. no one else knew what those stories were. To others, it was a memory, but they didn't live it, so they couldn't use the power. Moses staff of God and burning bush was dated at 1500 bc, so writing miracles on staffs and the rod of asclepion predates Moses. What these two ideas have in common is that they are symbols that stand for times when someone was in the zone. Or when you knew LIFE IS FOR YOU. You were the force that shifted sickness and health, lack into plenty, and enemy into a friend, fear into love. You are going to create your own symbols.

Your Distilled Power Journal

You want to get a journal that is of good quality. Something that feels good in your hands. Only write in it, good things that happened to you. Amazingly wonderful things covering your whole life. When a good thing happens- write it down. Only fabulous things. The Best. (You can put the other things in your gratitude journal.) Even One amazing moment can shift your life thirty or forty years later- that boost can turn the tide of events when you say it happened once, it can happen again.

These extreme moments are your guide when you are stuck or indecisive.

After some point, you will get an idea that you have power, you can give this a symbol, such as a sun or a bird or a tree – it is yours- it can be a rock with the word life on it. What ever it is, it is yours and it reminds you that you are that powerful. It has to be connected to your real life knowledge.

You may keep the symbol or revise it or have a whole collection. The important thing is to keep writing down those moments. As you do this, stronger buried power moment memories will surface- capture them! They are proof of your dominion.

Power Tools so far..

1. Directing to **God**
2. **Praising** is Raising
3. **Spiritual Vision.** There is a higher **Spiritual answer** inherent every problem.
4. **Transformation**
5. **Gratitude**
6. **Works**

7. YOUR LEVERAGE IS YOUR AUTHORITY:

AFFIRMATIONS

Why wait for Heaven?
Those who seek the light are merely covering their
eyes. The light is in them now. Enlightenment is but a
recognition, not a change at all.
A Course In Miracles

When we speak from the Christ within, our word has leverage. Sense your Christ within and allow it to speak through you these affirmations.

Say aloud

I am love

I am beautiful

I am Divine and Perfect because I am Goods Creation

I am whole and complete

I am unlimited radiant health

God made me with His own hands, and called me into existence: I am good and very good and am entitled to a grand inheritance of good.

I am wholly capable in any situation because I walk with a force of love that is greater than me.

I am blessed. I am prosperous. I am successful.

I am wise. I am happy I am healthy. I am in shape.

I an energetic. I am positive. I am passionate. I am strong.

I am confident. I am approved. I am secure. I am beautiful.

I am attractive. I am valuable. I am anointed. I am accepted. I am prepared. I am qualified. I am motivated. I am focused. I am disciplined. I am determined. I am patient. I am kind. I am generous. I am excellent. I am equipped. I am empowered. I am well able. I am a child of the Most High God.

Make up some I AMs and repeat them often! Sing them, dance with them, sing them in traffic, or when you are walking.

Our subconscious mind is a force to be reckoned with! It affects us even when we don't know it... usually when we don't know it. It has a HUGE part of play in our decisions (without an invitation) and its through affirmations that past programmed beliefs can be altered and future ambitions realized.

I am backed UP with unlimited power.

I am strong in the Lord and the Power of His Might.

All power is given unto me to bring my heaven upon my earth.

Now is the appointed time, TODAY is the day of my salvation.

Spiritual Power Tools

1. Directing to **God**
2. **Praising** is Raising
3. **Spiritual Vision.** There is a higher **Spiritual answer** inherent every problem.
4. **Spontaneous.** The Course in Miracles the very first principle states, "There is no order of difficulty in miracles. One is not harder than another, all expressions of love are maximal."
5. **Giving is receiving.**
6. **Gratitude** as a creative agent

7. **I AM what I AM**

8. ASK WHAT CAN I GET EXCITED ABOUT?

1. What's one thing I can get excited about? Ask this daily and see what changes.

In our early Pandemic Zoom Coffee Chat Question du Jour group, our first question du jour was, What can I get excited about? We asked ourselves this every day for a week and returned to our weekly meeting to discuss the question, what can I get excited about?

My whole energy system changed, when I thought about what I could get excited about and it led to many really simple things, simple but full of wellbeing. Planting flower seeds, cooking a Peach Dutch Baby.. it is a large peach pancake with an eggy batter. It fills the kitchen with the essence of vanilla pancakes butter and peaches. It was remarkable how one tiny question shifted my priorities. Doing things that supported my well being were not in my goals, but there was a yeaning and a space to do them. When we ask these empowering questions, our whole self shows up to lay a foundation for our well being. We are set up to not create from fear, but from a deep joy.

Try this.. what can I get excited about this week?

Which spiritual power tool is this for you? Faith? Praising?

9. INNER SINGING CHANT

Remember a melody that you sang as a child, like Twinkle, Twinkle Little Star…

What part of you is hearing the music? The music isn't present in the room, this is a part of intuition and imagination. They are linked. You can in your mind, stretch out the sound of the song, or make it staccato. This is creative. You are creative. This is called Inner Singing. You can use these gifts to transform your world by paying attention to how you use your imagination in a way that is unlike everyone else. This is to say, you cannot learn intuition in a book. You have to try something, and notice what happens, then you try something else, and you notice what happens. You begin to notice. You are not noticing when you are reading, but you can read slowly, and actually do some of the energy exercises if you slow down and create a space for the information to work in you.

I read somewhere that if your goal isn't scaring you it's not large enough. So, I joined the choir several years ago.

Seriously, I didn't think of myself as someone who can easily sing on stage. I used to think of myself as naturally off key and not a good singer (except in the shower or driving my car). I joined the choir to do something new, sort of a bucket list thing, and the idea of it scared me— being on stage with no singing talent.

The choir always looked like they were having such a great time up there singing songs of praise. They glowed! Could this happen to me? I didn't think so. Hitting the right key took a lot of practicing my scales during the week and learning about music. I'm just going to say this, if you don't think you can sing, you are not practicing your scales enough. You will learn with practice. (I'm convinced singing scales cleans out your chakras) Then there were the glorious songs which take you right to Source… I'll never forget one of the chants the congregation practiced,

> *I am so blessed*
>
> *I am so blessed,*
>
> *I am so grateful*
>
> *I am so blessed.*

We'd sing this over and over softly. When I first started, I wasn't so sure I was blessed, but sang along with everyone else. I sang it enough to where it became engraved in my mind somewhere, though, at times I was pretty sure I was cursed. That's how affirmations work.. At first the quote seems ridiculously impossible, but with repetition, the affirmation sticks and then it's a part of you. Around the time my dog died, I was in a sad place that turned into a doom and gloom depression. That chant came up, I wrenched that sweet little chant, until it moaned and sobbed. Then it was hilarious and my I laughed with tears streaming down my face. The worse I felt the funnier, and then pathetic it seemed. When we repeat affirmations they work through all the tissues of our body, emotions, mind, subconscious. When we repeat affirmations (or curses) they find the secret, buried, locked unloved places and work their magic. Our power is in our words and how they are used.

I am so blessed

I am so blessed,

I am so grateful

I am so blessed.

Sing this 10 times and see what happens. What does blessed mean to you?

Sing this over someone, anyone, just extend the idea.

You are so blessed

You are so blessed,

I am so grateful

You are so blessed.

Which spiritual power tools is this for you? Faith? Praising? Giving is Receiving?

Thank you to Rev. Queen Michele Jordan for the chant.

10. GOOD JOB!

Tell yourself good job. We don't validate ourselves as much as we can. No matter what you do, can you validate yourself, even if you screw up? We are here to learn and grow, and mistakes can mean we needed more information. If you punish yourself for making mistakes, growth can be stunted in some areas of your life. Also, at some point, every mistake will reveal something good later down the road, every mistake is actually about growth. Can you love yourself or say good job when you fail? Practice saying good job to yourself during the day. This is actually a really powerful to your inner being.

Would Praise be this powertool?

11. BEING AFFIRMATIONS

Just Be. Feel you beingness. Go within and breathe into the inner space of the Divine within, I gently let go of thinking and open to one life within me. I am now the

Living presence of my Higher Self within which is intimate with God. Source. The Life in all things is the life in me. I am one with the flow of Love, of Source. Breathe into life force. Breath into the consciousness that was here before time and is eternal. Breath into now. Notice now. Notice what now feels like. The past is blessed and all that remains is love. The future is in the hands of God and is better than I can imagine.

My divine presence now heals the past and future. In this holy moment, I am as God sees me, as God knows me. I am aware that the future is in Gods hands. This now moment is a holy moment. I take a vertical step in my consciousness to infinity. My heart is opening to more than I ever knew possible. As I open my heart, the Source of all life breathes more life into me. I am teaming with life force by letting go. I let go of any limitation, any idea that holds me back, any idea of lack in my life evaporates into the nothingness from which it came. Lack is not true. Sickness is not true. Truth is true and unchanging. I am true and timeless and loving and whole and complete and I notice this now. I may have thought I was sick or had lack but I was wrong. I was mistaken. I am Truth and truth is always well and vibrant health. I am peace. I am joy. I Am. I am one with One. Its limitless is mine. Its bounty is mine. I am guided by my intuition to always take a loving path. I let go of managing my intuitional system and allow my Higher Self to shine me in joy.

If you have any issue say, In terms of _____, there is nothing my holiness cannot do.

I notice the vibration of forgiveness, of atonement, of being forgiven, or given for by God.

Be whole, notice this, feel it. Know wholeness.

Be Love, notice this, feel this, Know Love.

Be Forgiven. Be wholly innocent!

Be wholly holy!

Be Christ Consciousness!

Be unlimited health!

Be amazingly wonderful! Say, I am amazingly wonderful!

Be perfection!

Be eternal joy!

Feel gratitude for your Self for animating your body. Which spiritual power tools is this for you? Can you see where this spiritual power tool is already happening in your life?

12. DEFINE YOUR ANSWERED PRAYER

If your prayer was answered, what would that be? What if your prayer was answered in a big, stylish, happy with grace Way? Can you go bigger? What would the ultimate answered prayer be? Can you daily write out your answered prayer? Would this be the Transformation Power tool?

13. MEDITATION

Another way of saying vibration is 'state of consciousness'. The more inner stillness we are conscious of, the finer our vibration becomes. Your state of consciousness is ridiculously powerful when you meditate. If you want to do only one activity in this book to create a better life do this one. Meditate. Find your local guru and start there. Your consciousness attracts every element of your life- Your dream fulfillment is a practice, not a destination. Heaven on Earth is accessed by your meditation practice.

What are states of consciousness and why do they matter?

States of Consciousness

Waking.
- Dreaming (REM sleep)
- Dreamless Sleep (non- REM)
- Transcendental Consciousness (TC)
- Cosmic Consciousness (CC)
- Glorified State of Cosmic Consciousness (GC)
- Unified State of Cosmic Consciousness (UC)

Why do states of consciousness matter? The higher thoughts you are conscious of— the more good you attract. It's like the bible saying seek first the Kingdom of God, all else shall be given. Our inner beliefs create our outer world. This idea is repeated in many cultures and faith traditions. Imagination is related to belief. When we begin to use our imagination and intuition to see ourselves as our creator sees us, we just create this idea, however imperfectly, that this is possible, a larger part of ourselves takes the next step, and something extraordinary shows up in life. You have to first make room in your belief system that this is possible. Your non belief will prevent and block. You open the door a little bit.. this could be possible.. just crack the door open that something exceedingly wonderful and beyond what I think is possible could happen, something deeply loving.. it could happen without delay, under grace with no effort on my part other than saying this is possible. This is our work. Crack that door open!

When we visit other states of consciousness by meditation we step out of our limited belief systems, out of karma, out of pain, and into pure potential.

We do not have to wait to die before we go to heaven, or be with the GodHead. If you are still and tell your soul to emerge, it will. If your mind is full of chatter you won't be aware of the presence. Gotta still those thoughts.

It's like your mind is a lake, the stiller it is, the more it reflects the sun. Can you still those waves?

These aspects of yourself must be invoke, invited, welcomed. The higher self does not interfere with your life.

It takes no effort. If you ask your Soul that was created by the hands of God and holds the thoughts of God to come forward, it must. It will in one holy second it will. It is only your mind that must make space- empty space for what is already there. This is why Mind is referred to as God. We can only allow what we are able to be conscious of. If you mediate a lot, you will discover you, your mind, your heart is actually a cathedral of the Living God. Pretty cool stuff!

Say hourly, something wonderful is happening…

Invoke wonderful and watch for it. Every time you see, sense, feel, wonderful… give thanks. Lean into gratitude for that back and forth communication with your soul and your outer life. You will create more of your dreams if you give thanks. The posture of gratitude is very creative.

14. TURN TO SOURCE, Again

When I say our creator, I mean the idea of Source, of the Supreme Being, Life, the Flow, the Force; and this is the force behind all forces, so it is the ultimate Good. We live in a world of duality, and cannot grasp an idea that lives outside of time and space. Mentally releasing limits of what you think this source is, you allow something greater into your mind and life. When you think of Source as something new, like: OOO, you create a space for a larger idea of who you are, perhaps as Omniscient, Omnipresent and Omnipotent. Dwelling on Omniscience expands your mind. All over the place, all over time, all knowing, you begin to intuit that there is no opposite power to Good. There is no evil, no bad, and no negative force in Good. If there is any idea of sadness, sickness, or death, it is non existent in Omnipotent Life. God is all Good and not a force of evil. As in the St. Francis prayer, we are using ourselves as an action of overriding fear by asking that we be an instrument of peace, or to be an agent of change in the world. It is in our giving that we receive. We stop being just a body and take up the talents and gifts of the soul.

Can you wrap your mind around the idea that all things in all ways are working for your greatest good? When we become aware of intuition and its insights, and feeling tones, we can also 'play' with that awareness, or imagine that the Source is part of it, and use our imagination and intuition to create. We can create anything, but when you add Good, or Source to the creation, you create win, win, win. You create better than you can imagine!

Edgar Cayce readings state that God desires to be expressed in the world through us. The example set by Jesus is apparently a "pattern" of wholeness for each and every soul.

Regardless of an individual's religious or personal beliefs, this Christ pattern exists in potential upon the very fiber of their being. It is that part of each of us that is in perfect accord with the Creator and is simply waiting to find expression in our lives. This Christ pattern was further described as "the awareness within each soul, imprinted in pattern on the mind and waiting to be awakened by the will, of the soul's oneness with God" (5749-14), and its manifestation is the eventual destiny of each and every soul. With this in mind, the readings present Jesus as our "Elder brother," a soul who came to show each one of us the way back to our spiritual Source by perfectly manifesting the laws of the Creator in the earth.

15. BEING TRULY HELPFUL

The Course in Miracles has a prayer that starts, "I am only here to be truly helpful." Not surface helpful.

When you are truly helpful, you are in a place where life cannot help but give back immediately.

Truly, freed from bondage, and walking out of the prison of limiting belief systems. Waking up from sadness, guilt systems, and 'can't make it' ideas to full freedom, full aliveness, full health, and strength to move blocks off your path. Full life force, full joy of living, sparkly eyes, and a shiny strong laugh no matter what is going on. It is my wish, vow, intention that the information in this book is truly helpful. Shine with all that God is in You, just for the joy of it. Let's shine together and on our world, and everyone in it and see, for a holy second, all of us sparkling with the light of love.

> *Lord, make me an instrument of your peace.*
> *Where there is hatred, let me bring love.*
> *Where there is offense, let me bring pardon.*

Where there is discord, let me bring union.
Where there is error, let me bring truth.
Where there is doubt, let me bring faith.
Where there is despair, let me bring hope.
Where there is darkness, let me bring your light.
Where there is sadness, let me bring joy.
O Master, let me not seek as much
to be consoled as to console,
to be understood as to understand,
to be loved as to love,
for it is in giving that one receives,
it is in self-forgetting that one finds,
it is in pardoning that one is pardoned,

I would like to add that we can be raised to eternal life right here and now. The dying referred to may be the dying of the ego. The Ego is the self who is never content, and plays the victim game. We are already ALIVE with our Eternal Spirit Now, because your eternal spirit cannot die. Its up to you to become aware of it. This awareness is called your spiritual path. Your spiritual path is your path towards your eternal spirit. You are never not on your path! Even in your darkest moment, doing your biggest screw-up, or sinning like crazy, you are still on your path! In fact, you can call your biggest screw-ups holy because the more physical, emotional, psychic pain you are in the sooner and more wholeheartedly you'll turn to the God of your Heart. Pain is truth pushing error out.

You will know when you are woke and when you are

walking dead. When we take on the St. Francis prayer, there is no sin or punishment for sin. We are, on our base level, creations of Good, and therefore have within our minds, the song and light of Creation before this planet existed. We are that I AM, innocent, never sinned, never failed, never fit into a tiny box, we are beyond our comprehension. And it feels good. Which power tool is this one?

16. IMAGINATION

See a rose in your minds eye. Notice the petals, how open the rose is, what color.

If you can imagine a rose, how do you imagine... what is seeing or knowing? These are inner abilities that everyone has.

"Imagination is more important than knowledge. For knowledge is limited to all we now know and understand, while imagination embraces the entire world, and all there ever will be to know and understand." ~ Einstein

See your Rose. Smell it. Notice how open it is, or what color the rose is. Your inner abilities are seeing the rose. Are you aware that intuition is as simple as seeing a rose with your mind's eye? Your decision to see a rose, and the imagination it takes to create it in your mind are part of your inner abilities. Intuition flies out the door when reason shows up. You cannot reason this imagining. Even if you say you aren't intuitive, you are! You learn a lot by just agreeing to try, and seeing what happens. Your intuition is telling you about your state of being by what the rose looks like. Does it need water? Is it radiant and healthy or frail? Ask the rose what it would like. Ask it to dance.

17. PLAYING WITH ENERGY

When you are in an awfully slow line, like a slow line at the post office (grocery store?) that is claustrophobic and not moving, notice what chakra others are in.

When you are in a church or spiritual center, notice what chakra people are in. Get a sense of the major belief systems in a group.

The lower the chakra the more body awareness and the higher, the more spiritual information they are using.

Here's a clue, you are probably in the same chakra you

notice others are in. It is okay. Don't change to another chakra, just notice. This is a good thing to notice when you are in a church or meeting or a stuck line you must be in. From which chakra is the leader speaking? Are they able to teach from their upper chakras or Spiritually? Are they reaching their congregation from a body level? What's going on? If there is a 3rd chakra game going on, you can help your relationship with it. I say this because what we see, is generally what we are. So.. go along..

A third chakra game is a control game, it is competition, who is the best at slowing the line down? Or it is a master/slave game. Can you be amused at this? If not you're the slave.

Notice if you are in amusement.

Jesus rose from death because he lifted his vibration. Rising up is raising your energy level so you can do works. You cannot work energy unless you are in a higher energy. You must be in amusement or higher, such as enthusiasm, that is why we do fake amusement, which will take you soon to amusement. Can you do a fake opera laugh.. you can laugh to yourself, or a Santa Claus ho, ho, ho? Just keep at it till you shift. At first you will be pissed off, ho, ho, ho.. ho, ho, ho. Keep at it till you understand you must laugh. You are changing energy of a bunch of lemmings who are in agreement to lower energy, or you are in lower energy because you are not conscious that you can change your vibration. It takes one person to change the energy of a room. One aware thought to wake up a room.

But, before we do that.. it's kind of fun to play with the energy. You will know when you're doing it right. The line will move, or someone in the stuck line will turn around and smile at you for no reason.

If you have taken spiritual based classes, taught classes, prayed, meditated, then you know that you are a spirit in a body. Most people, Emmet Fox says, MOST PEOPLE are walking dead. Emmet Fox used that term. It's extreme. The walking dead have no spiritual awareness and do not care to even learn what it is. If you are sensitive to energy then it is up to you to evolve the energy around you. This is yours to do, and the world needs you right now. So, next time you are stuck in a line get really excited, because with practice, you will be able to move energy and things will shift. Do not brag on this!! Don't tell a soul.

And if it's a stuck line, or even a traffic jam, people don't know any better, if it is a stuck meeting, or an enslaving meeting, this is really fun and a great time to 'play energy'.

The thing is, everyone will be grateful to you for liberating them from stuck energy. If you did not move the energy, **you will have amused yourself** while waiting in line.

Ground the room, see a box 12 inches in front of you in your minds eye, call it the room, ground it, and connect it to God. See a very bright light, call it God, you are postulating, this is Gods light, Ground the room and connect it to God.

Something will move if you do this in a state of amusement. It may be that you experience the room in a different way. **Your vision of the room changed.** You did nothing to those around you, you just change the way you see the room, with God!

You can try this with a traffic jam. Remember, there is no order of difficulty in miracles, right. One is not larger than another, all expressions of love are maximal.

WE created the world that we are experiencing. We can reset! The natural world is an image. The real world is spirit. **You will prove this when in the middle of defeat, you raise your energy to enthusiasm and declare Truth: God is flow. God is things working. God is supply.** I can't make you believe, you must do works and know for yourself.

Remember the ha, ha, ha exercise? This is why you learn amusement or fake amusement. When you want to work energy, you need to be in a high vibration or it won't work. When you are surrounded by boredom or apathy – you sometimes don't even realize it has brought you to its level of uncreation. That is why you need fake amusement and to practice it, so your energy can be high enough to create.

You have to be amused, a little detached, or neutral. It's hard to be neutral when you are pissed off and stuck in a line that is going nowhere, like at the Post Office. That is why fake amusement. Fake amusement makes energy working fun and easy and quick! It takes less than 10 seconds to ground a room and connect it to God. If it takes longer, you are not in amusement. You start where you are, and learn from what happens wonderfully. You will notice that you are one with the people around you, and there will be a joyous feeling.

If the line still isn't moving, or there is anger in the room, pack the room with angels. You are not making another angel jealous, you are not taking away from anyone else. Angels are Gods arms. There are unlimited angels. Pack the room with angels, knowing there is no order of difficulty in miracles.

Another thing. And this is for those who are pretty much ascended, you will understand this and the other readers will be lost. Not really lost, because in the back corner of their soul, they know this: The reason there is no order of difficulty in miracles is because we create the world as we know it. It is a reflection of our consciousness. The beginning lessons of a course in miracles show you this is true. If you don't want the stuck line, then do your meditation practice and prayer practice and you will not attract stuck situation into your life. If you did, and it is painful, then it is yours to bring God to. Every situation in the world, every problem is actually one problem and every answer can be boiled down to one answer. It is either a Call to God or it is God.

18. SAY HELLO TO THE UNIVERSE

If you say hello to the Universe, you'll eventually find something sending a ping back. What shows up is in the form that speaks personally to you, and in a form that is joyful.

In Conversations with God, Neale Donald Walsh writes:

"I have heard the crying of your heart. I have seen the searching of your soul. I know how deeply you have desire the Truth. In pain have you called our for it, and in joy. Unendingly have you beseeched Me. Show Myself. Reveal Myself.

I am doing so here, in terms so plain, you cannot misunderstand. In language so simple, you cannot be confused. In vocabulary so common, you cannot get lost in the verbiage.

So go ahead now. Ask Me anything. Anything. I will contrive to bring you the answer. The whole universe will I use to do this. So be on the lookout; this book (Conversations with God) is far from My only tool. You may ask a question, then put this book down. But watch.

Listen.

The words to the next song you hear. The information in the next article you read. The story line of the next movie you watch. The chance utterance of the next person you meet. Or the whisper of the next river, the next ocean, the next breeze that caresses your ear—all these devices are Mine; all these avenues are open to Me. I will speak to you if you will listen. I will come to you if you will invite Me. I will show you then that I have always been there.

All Ways."

This passage is from the book jacket of, Conversations with God by Neale Donald Walsh. This is a wonderful book for further reading.

19. FAITH AND VICTORY

I just watched the French open and this woman was down a set with Serena Williams, the number one seed. Yet the woman skipped between points and was full of joy. She made a point of displaying her joy to the crowd, even though she was probably not going to win if you looked at the score. Most tennis players would be breaking their racket, cursing, scolding the umpire when Serena is in her game, but Serena's opponent skipped like a happy carefree girl. She could not be broken and ended up winning the match. It was visible by her body language that her mind had already decided how she was going to show up in this match, and she did not let the effects of this world, the score, two sets down, and Serena's grunts, 95 mph serves, genius and power on the court, shake her in the least.

Think about it. Competition means someone is going to lose. We are on this planet with a win/lose mentality and this is how scarcity works. Scarcity says there is a limit, two players – they cannot both win. But here was this woman overflowing with joy as if she had already won— that Serena was not going to dictate how she felt at the moment. You get the sense that even if she had lost, she would rejoice. She would not be broken; the won or lost game did not define her. Winning or losing becomes less important than understanding you're in the middle of a competitive game. When we stop playing with the limits of competition and begin to use spiritual cooperation there is a major shift. The goal of winning at any cost is less appealing than the goal of playing our best no matter what the score.

We have all these inner abilities and levels of intuition, which can affect our outer world to various degrees. Your deepest beliefs create your existence, so to really change the outer effects such as your life situations, work, career, relationships, love life, and money, home, car, free time; you need to go really deep to change your core concepts. These show up as habits and can be seen as patterns that last for years.

So many things program us. We are moved and motivated by so many lexicons in our culture, and we are unconscious to the urgings that motivate how we spend our time, and work hard for things that are just programming.

For example, how a mother felt about her body, is projected onto her children, if a father's fathers father was a violent alcoholic, ideas and thought patterns are passed on for generations until someone changes that inward story of what is possible. Our whole culture is saturated with the idea that disease is hereditary. This is just an idea, that doesn't need to be true. But medicine will operate on unsick bodies, taking this or that out because there is a predisposition, because medical science says so, when this is just programming. This is not to say don't go to the doctor if you feel you are sick. Go to the Doctor and take care of yourself! Just consider that medical doctors cure causes and not always root issues. A mental healing, an energetic healing can remove dark energy before it manifests into a serious illness.

You can also talk to your problems.

You can say, Problem, you look huge and the whole world can say, you will defeat me, but I'm going to stay in faith and declare victory and believe. This problem is not a set back, but a set up for something great to come into my life. I will come out better and stronger! *You don't use your precious energy to give life to the problem.*

20. POSITIVE CORE BELIEFS

Scientific studies have proved that we have the ability, with meditation, with intention, affirmations, social connections, expression, play, **to change how the cells act in our bodies.** If you really want to see how programming is affecting you, look at your core beliefs. You can change your diet all you want, or things on the surface, and limited change shows up, but if your core belief is that the universe in against you, or mean, or meaningless, it's like swimming upstream. You do all this work and then nothing happens. Core beliefs are hidden, deep, and deeply engraved.

If your core belief is that **the universe is safe, abundant and helpful,** your life is on a joyful trajectory. An example of a core belief is how you feel about existence. Is your universe friendly, safe and abundant?

We carry ideas about who we are and why we are here from our ancestors, or from situations, society, education and more. Race belief. If you believe you are a victim to circumstances, this will show up in many outer forms, getting sick, stuck, needing certain drugs, identifying with a social group that isn't healthy, not finishing things, not completing school or projects that matter, or staying with an abuser. At the back of these thoughts is an idea that this is all I get because of _____ fill in the blank. Not worthy, doomed, sinned, if 'a' then 'b', these ideas are often from those around us – they are not even our ideas, they belong to the Gestalt of our culture.

Is your universe **safe, abundant and friendly**? Is everything working for your good? Is good loving? If you had a sit down conversation with Good would it be a loving conversation? Does Good look at you as His Greatest Achievement? Is that Good shining the whole Kingdom of Heaven to you every second of every day? What if this were true? If this is true, then the only blocks to abundance are in our mind. We can access only so much of our mind, and then there is the subconscious mind and its hidden belief systems. So, what if the subconscious was just like a computer; it only does what it is told to do. It goes on creating as if it was programmed, but if you change the programming or get an upgrade, you have a different result.

Remember in the 1970's when men went to the moon? Do you remember those computers? They took up whole huge buildings. Now an iPhone has more capabilities than those building-sized computers that sent men to the moon. Our minds are more than computers, much more powerful and creative. Using our whole awareness is like what happens when you begin to create **vertically instead of horizontally.** Or, as Deepak Chopra says, "the more we go to Source, the more power we have." **The universe corresponds to the nervous system looking at it.** If you are operating off of your eternal soul, your world is full of coincidences, miracles, and you are aware that the universe is talking to you every second. The more we get to the subtle essence or our deepest self, the more peace, love and unity we feel because it is Truth. The more we exist in Truth, and consciously are Being in truth, what is not true ceases to exist. So if I say what is bad, sick, sad is unreality, and does not exist, sadness, sickness and defeat may show up in your world as a fact. And when you pull your belief out of the idea that sadness, sickness and defeat need to stick around and take over, that something wonderful can and will show up instead; soon a new trajectory is created. You may recall the saying, "If a tree fell in the woods, and no one was there to see it fall, it didn't fall." This is a stretch, I know, but we are acknowledging facts and going to a deeper truth here.

21. DRESS REHEARSAL

'The mind that worries is doing a dress rehearsal for the thing they are worrying about.' ~ Dr. David Bruner

Write out and practice a dress rehearsal for your Very Best Case Scenario in finance. What does that day look like? Where do you go? What are your conversations like. What does love feel like?

(What are you doing now that is attracting or repelling the right amount of money into your life.)

Can you imagine or do a dress rehearsal for your Very Best Case Scenario in health? What does your energy feel like? What activities are easy for you? How are your relationships?

Do a dress rehearsal for your Very Best Case Scenario in relationships. What is the base feeling tone you have after speaking to someone? How are you called to serve?

Do a dress rehearsal for your Very Best Case Scenario in personal life. What is precious and abundant for you? What does your day look like?

Do a dress rehearsal for your Very Best Case Scenario in finance.

Do a dress rehearsal for your Very Best Case Scenario for your legacy. Imagine 100 years form now and it is the end of you life. You are on the stage of life and you hear applause and see people, thousands of them and they are thanking you for helping them.. What are they saying? Can you tune into your divine mission for this life?

$E=mc^2$ proves that energy is equal to matter. That matter and energy are interchangeable. So when quantum mechanics says that light is a wave and also a particle-both are true.

Quantum mechanics found when a scientist looked at light he saw a particle, and another scientist looked at light and she saw a wave. What they discovered is that **what you are looking for influences what you find.**

Quantum Mechanics says that just ***noticing something changes its existence.*** Science has proved that DNA strands can be changed by thoughts and meditation. We are living in a world where time does move faster, and we are beginning to become aware of how to manipulate time, energy and space with our thoughts. The fact is that there is more love on planet earth, you would never know it by the news, which gets to publish what ever it wants no matter how bloody and violent and without any warnings. Movies have to at least rate their violence, but not the news; even Facebook can show live videos of the latest horror in graphic detail and without editing. Even so, the fact remains, there is much more Love on our planet and this is taking everyone into a higher vibration, more power, more instant manifesting, and more compassion. There are statistics that prove this. There is much less world wide violence than even 30 years ago.

The news distorts the ratio by not showing all the peace and goodness that is relative to the shocking news they are showing. If the news spent equal time, for every awful thing, showing spontaneous healing, people waking up from coma's and going into full remission and health, couples reuniting and forgiving and growing in love, etc. you would see that the good more than outweighs the bad. If the news spent some time looking at how people are changing and growing, refusing to look at negativity and only focusing on the positive aspects of situations, the real stories and truth would emerge. What we focus on grows because our minds are always creating. If, when any situation occurs, if you can shift your way of looking — "I am in earth school and am here to learn and grow into the divine Being that I AM. What am I learning in this situation, how am I growing?" You instantly put yourself on a healing track because you are no longer co-creating the negativity.

That anxious mind can go in the *opposite* direction into faith and positive imagination. Worry and anxiety is faith used negatively. Worry is an aspect of imagination. We are imagining this life, did you know you are projecting the whole thing? You are the I AM! You are not your emotions, your feelings, you are not a body, you are LIFE itself!

22. AMUSEMENT

The Course in Miracles says, **"Into eternity, where all is one, there crept a tiny, mad idea, at which the Son of God remembered not to laugh. In his forgetting did the thought become a serious idea, possible of both accomplishment and real effects.
[T-27.VIII.6:2-3]**

The world, therefore, seemed to become a very serious idea because we forgot to laugh it away. A Course in Miracles (ACIM) gives us the means to remember to laugh at it, and realize that our real self has never left the Mind of God.

Are you abundantly provided for as you follow your path? What does abundant mean?

When I say this, you are thinking and probably not visioning this. There is a general knowingness that is not vision. There is a feeling tone associated with abundance, or even radiance. Knowing is light and understanding.

23. ANCIENT WISDOM

Let's look at Plato's chair in 423 BC. Plato ascribed more significance in the subjective than the objective when he asked, "What is chair"? He suggested that all chairs in the physical realm are imperfect variations of the ideal chair that exists in the subjective realm completely.

Plato said these things:

"Every heart sings a song, incomplete, until another heart whispers back. Those who wish to sing always find a song. At the touch of a lover, everyone becomes a poet."

We are armed twice if we fight with faith.

We can easily forgive a child who is afraid of the dark. The real tragedy is when men are afraid of the light.

"Music is a moral law. It gives soul to the universe, wings to the mind, flight to the imagination, and charm and gaiety to life and to everything."

24. ST. AUGUSTINE

I'm bringing up famous historic philosophers to point out how seeped we are in communal ideas. Medieval theories of moral reasoning have their origins in the moral theology of St. Augustine born in 350 AD, and the rational ethics of Aristotle 322 BC. Until the thirteenth century Augustine's responses to questions concerning free will, predestination, the nature of goodness, and divine freedom dominated moral speculation in the Latin West.

St. Augustine's ideas have been around so long they are in our DNA.

"Faith is to believe what you do not see; the reward of this faith is to see what you believe." St Augustine

"The truth is like a lion. You don't have to defend it. Let it loose. It will defend itself."

"To fall in love with God is the greatest romance; to seek him the greatest adventure; to find him, the greatest human achievement."

"One loving heart sets another on fire."

"The world is a book, and those who do not travel read only one page."

"Symbols are powerful because they are the visible signs of invisible realities."

"Order your soul."

25. DESCARTES

Rene Descartes, a philosopher in the 1600's, had a different idea. He said, 'I think, therefore, I am'. He agreed, yes, the universe is ordered, but a person's mind is chaotic and unpredictable, therefore, Mind has its own laws and the world of matter and form has its different set of laws. This is called duality. On the one hand, **Descartes** argues that the **mind** is indivisible because he cannot perceive himself as having any parts. On the other hand, the **body** is divisible because he cannot **think** of a **body** except as having parts. Hence, if **mind and body** had the same nature, it **would** be a nature both with and without parts.

A Cartesian model is something like, the nature of the universe is orderly, predictable and explainable, and it is not chaos. The universe is a mechanical model of everything- all things in matter and form are predictable, the sun revolves around the sky, and comes up every day. But the *mind* could not be justified in the same way, because the mind is chaotic and has its own way. This is the same as duality. Mind is different than matter – the world is predictable, but the mind is not. So, he goes further than St. Augustine, who says we are only a body and fated. Now, we are a body which is fated and in the world of form and a mind which has no rules at all, or our mind is unlimited and therefore like Source. We are both: Duality!

"I think; therefore I am." Rene Descartes

"I'm like a medium between God and nothingness"

"Whenever anyone has offended me, I try to raise my soul so high that the offense cannot reach it." Rene Descartes

26. NEWTON

In 1665, Isaac Newton had to work from home when the University of Cambridge temporarily closed due to the Bubonic Plague. It was the most productive period of his life and he used that time to develop theories on calculus, optic and gravity.

Newton developed the laws of motion and the theory of gravity. He also made discoveries in optics – a theory of colors – stating that the white light is a composite of all colors of the spectrum.

Isaac Newton gave rules to predictability with the apple falling and gravity, and his equations of gravity created the way for a man to be on the moon. Science could predict where the moon would be in its orbit, so they could land there.

Newton quotes:

No great discovery was ever made without a bold guess. To every action there is always opposed an equal reaction.

We build too many walls and not enough bridges.

The more time and devotion one spends in the worship of false gods, the less he is able to spend in that of the True One.

"You have to make the rules, not follow them." – **Isaac Newton**

"Truth is the offspring of silence and meditation. I keep the subject constantly before me and wait 'til the first dawnings open slowly, by little and little, into a full and clear light." — **Isaac Newton**

As a blind man has no idea of colors, so have we no idea of the manner by which the all-wise God perceives and understands all things.

27. ARISTOTLE

Aristotle was a Greek philosopher and polymath during the Classical period in Ancient Greece. He was the founder of the Lyceum and the Peripatetic school of philosophy and Aristotelian tradition. Along with his teacher Plato, he has been called the "Father of Western Philosophy"

We get the word metaphysics from Aristotle, and it means *what comes after physics.*

You can get a sense of the information in this book is nothing new, if Aristotle had this knowledge.. and they had all sorts of gods and goddesses back then.

 The ability to transform out thoughts is in our DNA. Here are some of Aristotle's quotes.

Courage is the first of human qualities because it is the quality which guarantees the others.

Fear is pain arising from the anticipation of evil.
It is during our darkest moments that we must focus to
see the light.

The actuality of thought is life.
The proof that you know something is that you are able to
teach it.

28. EMMA CURTIS HOPKINS

The average life expectancy was 45 in 1870 when Emma
Curtis Hopkins lived and cured many people with her
Scientific Christian Practice

In the 1880's there was no penicillin, people did not
know to wash or sterilize cloths they used to stop blood
flowing. For example, a person with a cut, or who had an
amputation (popular in that time), or experienced
childbirth, a cloth was used. But they didn't know to use
and impeccably clean cloth!!! Dirty cloths with germs
and viruses were used to stop flowing blood, delivering
chaos into the patients bloodstream eventually leading to
sepsis.

Sepsis, which is when the organs stop working, due to
casual use of sterile technique, remained the cause of half

the total deaths until 1937.

Bloodletting was so common, barbers did it, and that's why the barbershop pole has a red and white stripe. Red symbolizes the blood and white symbolizes the cloth. They had no idea the cloth had to be clean!!

I can see why you would want to use natural healing in the 1880's. If you were sick back then, your chances using Emma Curtis Hopkins method was better than bloodletting and dying of sepsis! Now we insist you use medical doctors when you are sick, that being said, Emma's technique is a key to spiritual healing, and it was so potent, every major contemporary New Thought organization can be traced directly to Hopkins's teachings. Still being used!

Emma Curtis Hopkins was called the "teacher of teachers," because a number of her students went on to found their own churches or to become prominent in the New Thought Movement. Among her students were Charles and Myrtle Fillmore, founders of the Unity School of Christianity; Malinda E. Cramer, co-founder of Divine Science; and considerably later Ernest Holmes, founder of the Church of Religious Science.

These are Emma Curtis Hopkins words:

"To be wise is to be in a perfect condition, for the without must be as the within. They who are wise do not speak of disease or pain or weakness or trouble, because they know that these things are not evidences of truth, but of false thoughts; foolish and ignorant beliefs. The wise only tell truth at all times, so they show out Truth and their bodies become spiritualized, sound, firm, hardy and enduring.

They breathe Spirit and lean upon Spirit for strength and vigor, and know that need only God to support and sustain life. The give no attention to heat or cold, to food or drink, to money or friends, but seek first the kingdom of God and all these things are added.

They speak the truth about strength, vigor and courage, no matter what appears; no matter how much weakness and feebleness seem to be true, for they know that these are but proof that strength and vigor are within, pushing out the untrue, unreal condition.

Weakness and feebleness are evidences of ignorance and foolishness, when we see anybody in that condition, we must deny ignorance and foolishness, saying, "you are not weak or feeble, you are not tired, or exhausted or languid. I refuse to acknowledge that you are suffering the consequences of the past or present foolishness and ignorance of your parents, or of the whole race—mind; you are not suffering the consequences of the foolishness and ignorance of the people around you; you are not suffering the consequences of your own foolishness and ignorance; you are not suffering for my foolishness and ignorance, for I am not foolish and ignorant at all.

God is your life; you cannot be threatened with death, nor fear death, nor yield to death.

God is your health; you cannot be threatened with disease or sickness ever.

God is your strength; you cannot be threatened with weakness, nor fear weakness, nor yield to weakness at all.

God is your peace; you cannot be threatened with discord or inharmony, nor fear discord or inharmony, nor yield to discord or inharmony ever. You are perfectly sound and well in every part.

You are alive with the life of the Spirit; you are bold with the boldness of Spirit; you are strong with the strength of Spirit.

You trust in God.

You are alive and strong and vigorous and hardy; energetic and bold and sound and well—*and you know it.*"

This is from Spiritual Law in a Natural World, by Emma Curtis Hopkins, a must read book.

29. LET THEIR BE LIGHT!

In Genesis, when OOO said Let there be light, she meant let there be understanding. Light is understanding. When you intend to understand, you will understand. Learning is adding to what you already know. If you already have a platform of spiritual understanding and/or a meditation practice, the words in this book will mean a different thing to those who are new to both. That doesn't mean there is no understanding – you start somewhere and that is- from where you are.

When you read, if you allow yourself a place in your mind and heart, to really relax into to the words and allow the deeper meanings to come forward in your consciousness you will remember Who you Are. The fact is, you are all Truth, and all Knowledge, and there is a part of your mind that never left Good's Mind. One of the purposes of this book is for you to **Remember Who You Are.**

So, when OOO, said, let there be light, and there was light, this is an invocation and a declaration that you yourself make a place for understanding to occur; You are Light. Let You Know Yourself. The veil drops and vanishes at your beckoning. Understanding will show up in time, but your beckoning, and the passion and deep invitation brings revelation and the great peace that is Divine Knowledge now.

Remember, enthusiasm comes from entheos, which means in God, Theos is God in Greek.

When you ask yourself, 'Who am I here to be? At the core of my being, what spiritual qualities am I here to be?' Just asking the question stirs and awakens your

MIND.

30. ARCHETYPE

Which archetype is standing in me now? Is the archetype of Christ too much? How about Athena, or Quan Yin? Their qualities are in you now, waiting for expression.

31. EXPRESSION

I often find those who can't change their energy are actually asking for a creative outlet and a practice. And then they easily transform at will because they have a creative practice that keeps them flowing. On the mortal side, we can be the effect of the world of disaster especially if you have a steady diet of news, or respond to those who are often complaining, "we're doomed, I'm too busy to meditate", and forget we have a choice. The energy behind dis-ease can be described as cells going crazy because their expression is blocked.

This quote from A Course in miracles, "Miracles transcend the body. They are sudden shifts into invisibility, away from the bodily level. That is why they heal," is not so mysterious when we consider the proverb:

"The body heals with play, the mind heals and laughter and the spirit heals with joy."

Exercise, journaling, dancing, singing, running, whatever it is that calls you is your Expression. It is allowing a flow, and when you let things out in other ways then we usually do, the unexpressed is no longer bottled and bundled up inside, tightening your muscles, attracting mental debris and clutter. Like a good conversation with Source, we have allowed expression. That is why artmaking is so healing. It isn't about the end product at all or making a good art-piece, or song, or a beautiful dance, it is more about the journey of surrendering and just playing, putting things together in an unscripted way, ugly or beautiful, it doesn't matter, we aren't judging we are letting loose. This is tremendously healing because it's allowing an unseen, elemental energetic flow, where hidden or subconscious aspects of our personality or soul are allowed to speak in their own wordless language.

When you write, sing or play, content often expresses what is not in your speaking mind.

When you paint, things speak in a language of color that has no other way to make itself known.

When you sing, the heart is allowed to communicate in a way that doesn't come in any other way but song.

When you free dance, you allow the body, and your spirit

to tell their (painful, tragic, crazy, messy) story, you are allowing expression and it is unrehearsed, it just goes, and that stuck energy is expressed out. It is not bottled up, seething, and warped, and becoming petrified and mutating, it is gone! We step away from our mental monkeys and become present in the flow of all of creation. Time can take another shape and disappear, but we are fully conscious.

32. GO PAST YOUR EDGE

Life begins on the edge of your comfort zone. We must really be alive right now. In this pandemic, we as a world are having to redefine our lives.

Expose yourself to your deepest fear, after that, that fear has no power. You are free.

"What is fear? What is a 'comfort zone'? And…if we took the time to turn the light on it, look at it, face it…would it go away?

Have you ever faced something that you were afraid of and…once you did, it either no longer intimidated you or you realized it wasn't anything to be afraid of in the first place?

When we realize the monster isn't there, the fear is immediately gone. The mind no longer has anything to feed on and to magnify.

The same applies with life. As we grow older, we often accumulate more fears and, if we don't 'turn the light' on them, they will marinate and magnify. The process of addressing our fears usually means that we need to do something that makes us feel very uncomfortable and often requires a resilience to push through…to push past great feelings of discomfort to come to the realization that…there is no monster and…suddenly realize how magnificent and capable we are. And…as a secondary win, our self confidence and love receives an immediate boost too.

As we work out this 'face your fears' muscle, we slowly start to welcome the journey to reach more, do more and achieve more and…often facing our fears becomes a challenging joy.

Why not invite yourself to write a list of your fears and commit to face one over the next couple of months. Chances are, that scary monster? Doesn't exist!

33. EXERCISE

Exercise is always a good idea. Emotion is tied to motion, so get moving.

A major and often overlooked benefit of exercise is that it helps you to sleep better. But the benefits of exercise don't stop there. Below are 100 other benefits of exercise (not necessarily in order of importance).

1. Reduces blood pressure
2. Reduces cholesterol levels
3. Increases the concentration of high-density lipoprotein (HDL or "good" cholesterol in the blood)
4. Reduces chances for coronary heart disease
5. Increases efficiency of heart and lowers resting heart rate
6. Makes heart muscles stronger
7. Improves contractile function of the heart
8. Strengthens lungs
9. Improves respiratory function
10. Improves cardiovascular endurance and performance
11. Provides more oxygen to body, including organs and muscles
12. Provides more nutrient supply to the body
13. Reduces chances for stroke
14. Helps to alleviate varicose veins
15. Increases metabolic rate
16. Stimulates digestion
17. Makes digestion more efficient
18. Stimulates intestinal movements, resulting in better elimination of wastes
19. Reduces changes for colon cancer
20. Strengthens and develops muscles
21. Increases efficiency of muscles
22. Benefits joints due to stronger muscles
23. Helps maintain cartilage health in the joints

24. Eases muscular tension
25. Alleviates back problems
26. Increases muscle flexible and agility
27. Improves speed of muscle contraction and reaction time
28. More healthy skin due to the fact that skin pores open more during exercise, resulting in more efficient removal of dirt and impurities
29. Burns up and removes toxins from body
30. Increases blood flow to the brain
31. Stimulates growth of nerve cells in memory center of the brain
32. Improves various indexes of psychological functioning
33. Enhances brain functioning by increasing the amount of oxygen available to it
34. Increases sense of well being
35. Increases resistance to pain because endorphin levels are elevated
36. Increases sense of excitement because hormone epinephrine is elevated
37. Alleviates boredom
38. Lessens worry and tension
39. Reduces stress by removing lactic acid from blood
40. Alleviates anxiety and/or pain because tranquilizing effect of exercise lasts for several hours
41. Enhances mood
42. Reduces anxiety more effectively and safely than anxiety-reducing medication
43. Boosts energy

44. Improves self-esteem and self-confidence since body and mind are improved and strengthened

45. Increases sense of self control

46. Provides source of pleasure and fun

47. Releases anger and negative emotions

48. Reduces depression more effective than short or long-term psychotherapy

49. Enhances coordination, power, timing and balance

50. Boosts immune system functioning

51. Reduces severity of asthma

52. Improves functioning of organs

53. Can relieve tension headaches

54. Can reduce the urge to smoke because the adrenaline rush and stress relief from a brief workout can replace similar feelings smokers get from tobacco

55. Burns calories

56. Causes body to use calories more efficiently

57. Causes weight loss

58. Allows one to keep lost weight from returning

59. Can act as an appetite suppressant

60. Decreases fat tissue

61. Improves physical appearance

62. Enhances one's image and opinion of the body

63. Improves bone density and prevents osteoporosis

64. Reduces joint discomfort

65. Help manage arthritis

66. Allows one to feel better about their bodies and enjoy sex more as a result

67. Provides enhanced ability to achieve orgasm

68. Allows for greater sexual satisfaction

69. Can reduce or eliminate impotence due to increased

blood flow

70. Prevents or manages type 2 diabetes

71. Helps insulin work better, lowering blood sugar

72. Has a significant salutary effect on fibrinogen levels

73. Alleviates menstrual cramps

74. Improves athletic performance

75. Can add years to one's life

76. Enhances quality of life

77. Reduces pain and disability

78. Improves glycogen storage

79. Reduces risk of developing certain types of cancers of the colon, prostate, uterine lining and breast and other chronic diseases

80. Regulates hormones

81. Allows you to overcome illness or injury more quickly

82. Can lessen medical bills

83. Reduces anxiety by causing fewer worries about health

84. Can allow for better performance at work

85. Allows one to stay independent as they get older

86. Can keep health care insurance premiums lower

87. Makes one more attractive to potential mates

88. Allows for healthy pregnancy

89. Increases energy and ability to do things one likes

90. Allows you to be more productive and less stymied by stress and depression

91. Can help make possible increased income due to increased energy

92. Allows one to become more familiar with their body

and its functioning

93. Can stimulate mentally

94. Lets one eat more without gaining weight

95. Provides a healthy break from work

96. Adds variety and spice to life

97. Gives one increased ability to defend oneself and loved ones if needed

98. Provides a natural high afterwards, such as runners' high

99. Provides heightened alertness

100. Reduces inflammation

34. PRAY

A Course in Miracles says prayer is the medium of receiving light and miracles are the medium of dispensing of that light. Prayer is a form of communicating with our creator. The Lords Prayer gives a good example of answered prayer. If you notice how this prayer is worded, we are talking to our MotherFather Creator as if She/He is going to do everything we are asking. There is connection with food for our soul. The Word. The living waters of Christ. Notice the word our *daily bread.* This assumes we are already a part of God and that we going to get what we asked for. It is already ours. And notice we are saying, declaring actually as if all of mankind is entitled to our daily bread. We are at once, asking for everyone, united with all souls. This happens when we are meek, for some reason, and when we are sharing what we receive and when we give thanks and praise to the Divine Source.

A sanctuary in spirit. There is a sense in prayer. You may have your favorite prayer, so get to it and receive your spiritual food.

35. CREATE A SPIRITUAL MENU

If you could ask for daily food from God, or Universal Love or whatever you call the Entity who breathed life into you, who created you to have dominion over your mind. You know you can move a mountain of baloney anytime you want to. You can breathe life into ideas and projects you thought were dead. You can breath life into those who have given up. What do you need every day to keep your spirit boldly full of life? I mean overflowing radiantly full of enthusiasm and joy. Radiating this so much the Debbie Downers of your life cannot stand to be around you any more. Spiritual Food for the Hungry Soul, you can order any meal from Genesis to Revelation. The psalmist said in Psalms 119:103, How sweet are your words to my taste; sweeter than a honeycomb to my mouth. What is on your spiritual menu for the day?

Morning

Tune into Gods Love and say: I am Light, I am Life, I am

Supply (or your favorite quote)

Noon

Your favorite quote.

Evening

God is peace. I am grateful for all the good things that happened today.

Night time snack

I am wrapped in Gods love. I snuggle into Divine Presence.

36. CREATE SPACE FOR YOUR DREAMS TO COME TRUE

Healing is Mental as well as physical. You can work all you want on the physical side of things, and search outside of yourself all you want, but ultimately you are chasing illusions. For real change, get a vision from your Higher Self, Source, God, whatever you call It.

I'm using these words although; I have no idea what's going on. I just know that if you have a vision, a direction and it is from Divine Spirit, it will bring life, love and peace. It will be win-win.

When you begin to use your toolkit for success— at first you may be afraid to face your Creator. It could be you are afraid your past sins will be discussed. I can assure you the idea of sin is a man made concoction and Source can't understand sin, because it is not of Good. God only knows good, love, peace and joy. Or, why did Christ die for our sins? There is a sense that we can offer our troubles to the Lord and allow a spiritual idea that works better for us. Even if you can't yet imagine this, it's still true. Visioning becomes a way of forgiving ourselves, because the visions are as God sees us, so we are 'given for'. God is giving us a true idea instead of our false idea. And I say vision, but sometimes the vision is an idea, a feeling, a knowing, a word. This is the other dimension which is limitless, so words are too small for this communication. It is an inner awareness that sometimes cannot be understood, but we open the way for this when

I say 'Vision'. We are given the holy sight that our creator sees in us and in this our karma and sins are released, and we have a clear view on how to proceed with All of Heaven behind us every step of the way.

37. DRAW YOUR ANSWERED PRAYER

What does this look like? Play with variations and put images where you can see them.

38. CREATING A MEDITATION PLACE, AGAIN.

Where you are going to sit and imagine and pray, and receive communication from the Divine? This is a holy sacred place. You think this is taking time out of your day, but when you have clear guidance, you save lifetimes of time, you no longer do things that don't serve you, you move swiftly because you're sure footed. A meditation place can be a chair that has a straight back, a corner of a room, a whole room, it's just a place you create with the sole purpose of meditation. When you do this externally, you begin to internally create a place in your life for meditation. You want to meditate. You clean your room, your house, why not clean your mind? Why carry around a bunch of mental poop when you can have a clear fresh clean mind?

You want to meditate every day. Start for 5 minutes a day. If this is too much, create the space and fill it with things that remind you of extreme love. This could be a favorite blanket, a transcendent photo, or an image of you conquering something you thought impossible. It could be a color you like. The chair should allow your feet to sit flat on the ground. You want to allow your palms to be face up on your thighs.

You may want to get an inspiring book, or a sacred book, one you like. Or a few books that you like, some prayer beads, or images that remind you that there is a greater love.

You may want to create an altar. This lets you know physically you are in a sacred place.

I am sensitive to sound, and often when I start to meditate, airplanes fly overhead, and all of the sudden they are really loud. (Noisy airplanes were flying overhead before, but I didn't hear them.) Someone might start mowing the lawn nearby, you name it. After many attempts to move the sound elsewhere, or ground it, or erase it to no avail, I finally declared to the universe that I am in a sacred place. I tell the airplanes, 'This is a sacred place, be reverent!" and then go onto my meditation. I didn't change the sounds, I changed my relationship to meditation. Declaring a sacred space helps me to let go, and eventually the sounds diminish. Or I wear earplugs or headphones or both! Give yourself the power to insist on your inner time, and realize the more things that prevent you from going there, the more you need to do it.

It seems at times, the world does not want us to have our inner sacred sanctuary, and this is the very time we can say, with great softness and grace to the world, you do not boss me around, I will have my sanctuary! My peace was installed in my creation – meditation allows me to rediscover it.

After some time in meditation the outer world calms. The more jarred the outer world, the more it's time to meditate. We learn of our beautiful connection.

You may want a journal to capture some of the moments of revelation. You may want some crayons or markers to capture any images you see. Any words. Impressions. They are sacred.

Meditate in the same place daily, or when you can. This builds up an energy vibration. Each time you come to this place you make it easier to meditate. You can meditate in your work chair, it can be the same chair you dine in.

39. READ INSPIRING QUOTE AND BREATHE

To get started in you meditation space, you can read a passage that **inspires you.** Then sit with that passage and allow it to sink into an inner stillness.

I learned how to meditate when I was 12. At the time my sister was really into Transcendental Meditation and was close to Maharishi Mahesh Yogi. Because I was so young, I was to meditate for only 12 minutes instead of 20. Before meditation we'd do 30 minutes of asanas-these are yoga poses and then 5 minutes of pranayama, breathing exercises. Then we'd finally get to our meditation. I was given a mantra which was just a sound, it meant nothing. I just sat there staring at my naval, for years with mind numbing results.

Please aim for love from the start. I suggest meditation on the word love, or life, serene, grace, or peace. Repeat it, allow subtle qualities to unfold gently. You may use the word, Jesus Christ, or something from your personal religion – that inspires. We want an inspiring idea, that is loving and free. You can even say to yourself on the inhale, *L o v e* and on the exhale, *F r e e.*

This brings up a another point. As you begin to meditate, you may notice energy from the past, which may bring up bad memories, these will pass quickly as they are really nothing, and aren't you glad you're finally clearing that stuff away? Just keep aiming for Divine Love, or Peace, or what ever, just keep a goal to turn your mind to *inner divine presence*. Turn your mind to your heart. This is why most people learn meditation from a teacher. There is some energetic guidance. If someone already has the practice of light, it's a lot easier to learn from them. Your energetic body learns very quickly. Just own your soul and don't let it be mandated by ideas that are not of love and freedom. It's your soul, no one owns your time here on earth. As you do this enslavement to false ideas and problems you are yoked to will be broken and you will be yoked to truth.

Your goal is to be in the heart of love.

You do not need a guru, you many want to learn from another lineage of spiritual teachers. There is some female hatred in the guru line of teaching. I say this because some of us are women and when there is a spiritual group that does not allow women to be a guru or a priest, it tells women in a subtle way, we don't have the right to go directly to God. We need a male guide to access our full divine right.

Here is a story that you will not hear from the gurus. The following story illustrates that we as women are powerful to change things. And we cannot rely on male traditions to teach us.

In 1870, my ancestor, Ida Scudder was born into an American family of medical missionaries who lived in India. Her father was a doctor and practiced in a village in India. One evening, teenage Ida was confronted by a man who begged her to come and save his wife who was apparently dying in childbirth. She had no medical training, she was practically a child. She asked her father to come and save the dying woman, but it was explained that he, by law, could not treat a married woman. Ida was horrified, when another man arrived, banging on her door, screaming, demanding that she come and save his wife, which hurt Ida even more. She felt, if there was only something she could do! Another man came with the same demand, the same wailing. They stared into her eyes and begged and pleaded.

One night, three dying women, three helpless men looking to her to save their beloveds and Ida was powerless to act.

At that time, not so long ago in India, men were not allowed to touch another mans wife, **therefore *no medical care was given married women for any reason.*** Since Ida's father was a well known doctor, the men in the village assumed Ida had the same knowledge. The law was, a female could treat another mans wife, but never a male. But females were not allowed to become doctors. Three times that night, young Ida heard the death drums and the wailing and felt shaken to her soul. Her father could do nothing. Ida had no idea what to do, she was practically a child with no medical training.

When Ida saw this injustice she left the good life of a debutante and worked hard, busted through male strongholds and became the first woman to graduate from Cornell medical college in the US. **Ida then opened the Mary Taber Schell Hospital in India in 1902.**

Realizing that it would be impractical to go on alone in her fight to bring better healthcare to South India's women, she decided to open a medical school for girls only - (Indian women could then not have to die from lack of medical treatment if doctors were female). Her decision was viewed skeptically by some and it was told that that Ida would have consider herself lucky even if she got at least three women applicants. On the contrary, Ida got 151 applications the first year (1918) and had to turn many away subsequently. At first, the Reformed Church in America was the main backer of the Vellore school, but after Dr. Scudder agreed to make it coeducational, it eventually gained the support of 40 missions. Of the 242 students today, 95 are men.

Later, it had become so well known, Mahatma Gandhi visited the medical school. In 1945, the college was opened to men as well as women. In 2003 the Vellore Christian Medical Center was the largest Christian hospital in the world, with 2000 beds, and its medical school is now one of the premier medical colleges in India.

The point of this story is this woman, used her common sense when she saw women were dying in front of their husbands because no man was allowed to touch another mans wife- even a medical doctor to save her life. Ida

Scudder stopped her luxury life to become a medical doctor so she could go back and save women in India who were dying for no reason.

India is where all these gurus come from and every guru had a guru who let millions and millions of women die for no reason. Just saying, yes, all this spiritual information comes from Guru's, but they are still imperfect if they would allow women to die for no reason because of stupid laws. If Gurus from India were so great, they would have changed the law and it wouldn't take a female American teenager to make things right.

Our Christian tradition has burned women at the stake because they forgot to hide their intelligence. Our Christian tradition has caused more death and dying than any other cause in the world.

My point is trust in the highest Love, the only supreme God, Christ means truth. Aim high.

You do not need a guru with all his lineage of rules, customs of you need to practice yoga and then do asanas and breathwork before you can reach the kingdom of heaven. It is not better in India. It's not better to earn every degree you can in a religion. The only guru is the God of your Heart. You have your way and it is unique. You are the Divine, the Universe with a body around it, you don't need some teacher to access your spiritual nature.

Be in the heart of love and unfold. Notice your consciousness as you do this. Focus intently on love till your seeped into Its dimension. Stay there.

40. GRATITUDE JAR

Daily write down things you are grateful for. You can have a gratitude journal, but a gratitude jar is fun. You cut out the passage and put it in a jar. When you are feeling blue, pull out a gratitude passage and read it.

41. DE CLUTTERING

This comes naturally, making room for things that match your peace.

42. ORGANIZING YOUR DRAWERS

Can you make an abundance drawer? What does it look like? Can you fill a drawer only full of things that make you crack up and belly laugh?

43. CONNECTING

All connections are God in your life. Can you see it that way? Even the worst relationship is still a holy encounter. Can you look at your worst enemy as see them as divinely sent? This is funny **only** after you have prayed and meditated.

44. LAUGHING YOGA

45. TAKE FOOD TO A HOMELESS PERSON

46. CATHERINE PONDER

EVERYTHING ABOUT CATHERINE PONDER IS ALL CAPS!

A PROSPERITY MEDITATION FOR GATHERING YOUR MANNA by Catherine Ponder

"WHEN I FIND MYSELF IN A FINANCIAL WILDERNESS, IT IS BECAUSE I AM PREPARING FOR A GREATER ABUNDANCE THAN I HAVE EVER KNOWN BEFORE. MY WILDERNESS EXPERIENCE IS MY DIVINE INITIATION INTO

THE HIGHER LEVELS OF SUPPLY. **I AM BEING FREED FROM ALL FEAR OF LACK.** AS I LOOK TO GOD FOR GUIDANCE AND SUPPLY, I AM BECOMING FINANCIALLY INDEPENDENT ON A DAILY BASIS.

"I CAN GATHER MY MANNA BY FIRST USING SOMETHING CLOSE AT HAND TO MEET MY NEED. BE IT EVER SO HUMBLE, WHEN I USE WHAT IS CLOSE AT HAND, MY GOOD MULTIPLIES. I CAN BEGIN TO GATHER MY MANNA BY DOING SOMETHING FEARLESS. THE ACT OF BLESSING WHAT IS ON HAND INCREASES IT MIGHTILY. SOMETHING MYSTERIOUS HAPPENS WHEN I BLESS THE SUBSTANCE AT HAND. INSTEAD OF ENVYING ANOTHER'S PROSPERITY, I OPEN THE WAY FOR INCREASED SUPPLY TO COME TO ME.

"SINCE WORDS ARE CREATIVE, I CAN GATHER MY MANNA THROUGH SPEAKING FORTH DEFINITE, RICH WORDS OF SUPPLY, EVEN IN THE FACE OF LACK. MY MANNA IS ALWAYS SOMETHING CLOSE AT HAND, AND I ALWAYS

HAVE IN MY IMMEDIATE MIDST WHATEVER IS
NEEDED TO BEGIN GATHERING MY MANNA. AS I
BLESS THE MANNA CLOSE AT HAND AND
FEARLESSLY USE IT, IT MULTIPLIES. LORD, I DO
GIVE THANKS FOR THE ABUNDANCE THAT IS
MINE NOW!"

47. WE ARE THE SUM TOTAL OF OUR THOUGHTS

If, during the day, you feel your energy dip, are trashing
yourself, are attracting trouble, and you aren't up to
practicing the VBCS, then read inspiring books, or
exercise or realize sometimes we shouldn't be visioning
when we are angry!

The reason I lay into God so much is I have practiced ego
based visioning and it teaches you quickly to stop it! If
you practice this powerful practice and don't have good
intentions, it will either give you a good quick lesson or
lead you to slow down.

Except the LORD build the house, they labour in vain
that build it: except the LORD keep the city, the
watchman waketh *but* in vain.

Psalm 127

Just reading a little before you go to sleep, or after your evening novel, a little affirming at lunchtime adds up over time. If you are watching a lot of news how are you balancing this? Collect your own books and affirmations so you will always keep the balance of your internal dialogue loving.

48. ABUNDANCE

So let's look briefly at the energetic substance of money. The dollar bill is an example of abundance. It is trust that a piece of paper is going to be backed by gold and energy will be circulated. The dollar is taken on faith that there is plenty of gold in the bank and that establishes the value of the dollar. The law of spiritual Abundance works the same way. When you shift your thinking from impossible to pay debt to knowing you can easily pay a debt off, your energy changes from lack to abundance. There is trust.

When you send thanks to your bill collectors for the valuable services that you received and really wallow in the goodness of what you received, then the flow circulates. What you give thanks for increases. When you see that the services were already given with faith that they could be easily paid for. (When you bought something you knew you would pay it off…) you are aligning with the energy of trust, or faith. You are actively putting your energy into what's working well instead of what is not working well.

The Lord's Prayer is a recipe for abundance if you look at the symbols behind the words. The bible stories are our stories of who we are and how we move in consciousness. We are the Moses, the Jesus, and the prodigal son as we move though the lessons of life. The Bible is a recipe book for alchemy. 'Give us this day our daily bread', when viewed with your Metaphysical super seeing glasses on can mean, give me my substance. Emma Curtis Hopkins writes,

> "Give me this day my super-substantial bread… our secret ego, our God-spark, our 'hidden man of the heart' .. must have the bread of heaven.
>
> Forgive us out debts is now understood to be, "Give for our emptiness, Thy Substance."

49. DOMINION

Sometimes when I was doing my yoga asanas, I would hear this voice telling me I had a certain disease whenever I came to a certain yoga pose. For years, I let that voice have its say, and sort of believed it because it came from within. Now I know better, in the same inner voice, I take dominion, and tell myself how radiantly healthy I am. How Good is perfect and because Good is who I am on the inside, therefore it is impossible that I be anything other than perfect health. Good is in every cell of my body, every particle of my mind, my aura is Good, my chakras are Good.

Say this until you are radiant.

Don't allow any idea that isn't up to snuff to define you, or tell you how it's going to be.

When you hear anything inside your mind or outside your mind like another person judging or criticizing you in any way, go right to declaring your truth- you are a wholly perfect creation of Good, and cannot be anything other than perfection! What another thinks of you is none of your business: read the Four Agreements. What someone thinks of you and how you are doing things is a reflection of THEIR mind. Do not allow anyone to put his or her issues on you. This isn't to say there are things you need to do, you can do them, and understand a criticism is only a reflection, and a guide, but a criticism is not an essential truth of you. So love is called for here. As you become aware of your inner state of perfection, you are helping others.

Your thoughts keep creating! All those thoughts you had in the past that you learned from while you were less evolved are still there. If you don't do something about those past thoughts, they will still create. You will have moved on, but you will have subconscious workings that are impossible to see- that is why they are unconscious or subconscious- that means you are not aware of them. In light working, Sanaya Roman says this is a myth, and actually has light working exercises where you see what's in your subconscious or unconscious mind and clean it up. This is to say that you CAN bring consciousness to subconscious beliefs. It is as easy as making I AM statements and affirmations.

50. IT'S ALL HERE NOW

Remember, the last step is in the first step, and make a

clear firm declaration: My whole being, every part of it is God. If it's not God (or truly loving) it does not exist. What is not of God goes back into the nothingness from which it came! God works in the now. Things do not have to take time unless you believe they do.

Your past does not exist. It is blessed. If you don't feel your past is blessed, then hand it to God for a blessing. All is transformed to Love. Your future is in the hands of God. It is blessed. Here and now.

51. AGAIN MEDITATION SPACE

A place in your home is your sacred meditation place when you add colors you like, textures you like, images, flowers, scents- this is indicative of your internal meditation space. It is symbolic. You may create this space by wearing comfy jammies and slippers. It is a comfy place, where you get to be you. A place where you can let go of all the things you are holding onto to please others. Let go of all the problems of the world, and simply be.

Energy flowing up and down your spine is good, so upright allows this. When you begin to meditate, you may become aware of all the energy in your life that does not want you to find your inner space. Phone calls from people you haven't heard from in ages; the neighbors start building a new wall, jackhammers, and loud noises. They all come up. Congratulate yourself when this happens and know this noise will come to a deep peace you have never experienced before with just a little practice. It is hard to comprehend how what is going on in your world is a reflection of your state of being. When you meditate, you are the calming agent. Find that pool or still lake in your mind, and notice if there are waves in the lake. Your attention is in the space between your eyes, and you can easily calm the whole system. That is why there is in the bible, if thine eye be single the whole body will be filled with light. You create the calm still waters. Breathing slowly, and counting 4 breathes in and 4 breathes out.

If the waves persist, then laugh. You are taking yourself too seriously. You can always calm the waters of your mind! That is why you do yoga before you meditate.

52 BREATH DEEP

Pranyama

Place the thumb and the index finger on the nostrils. Plug one side. Breathe in and out 3 times. Close the other nostril, and breathe in and out 3 times, switch and do this for 5 minutes. It will calm and balance your system.

You can also do and in and out breath for each nostril with the other nostril closed.

I was initiated into Transcendental Meditation with a grand ceremony with flowers and fruit when I was twelve years old. That year and a few years afterward, I went on retreats with Maharishi Mahesh Yogi in teleconferences. We studied the Bhavagad Gita, and listened to holy prayers sang by holy people. We would practice 12 yoga poses and pranayama before each twice daily meditation. We were supposed to breathe so slowly that we couldn't hear our breath, and allow this stillness to guide us to our finer existence. (a tall order for a 12-13 year old- but the seeds were planted) And we were to breathe deeply as possible, slowly as possible. This is an ancient technique passed on by yogis to yogis and it takes you to some sort of alpha state.

At age twelve I was also confirmed into a Christian Church, in the same church I had attended since birth.

Look back at your life around your liminal or transitional stages of growth, what were you doing? What seeds of growth are you planting now that will bloom many years later? Your meditation practice and prayers are planting seeds of love for your future.

It all starts with Being Still.

"Be still
Stillness reveals the secrets of eternity" ~ Lao Tzu

"Peace comes from within. Do not seek it without."

~ Buddha

"Space and silence are two aspects of the same thing. The same no-thing. They are externalization of inner space and inner silence, which is stillness: the infinitely creative womb of all existence." ~ Eckhart Tolle

"Silence is the great teacher and to learn its lessons you must pay attention to it. There is no substitute for the creative inspiration, knowledge, and stability that come from knowing how to contact your core of inner silence." ~Deepak Chopra

"We can never obtain peace in the outer world until we make peace with ourselves." ~ Dalai Lama XIV

When you begin to meditate regularly, you are changing your whole belief system and for the victims, there will a thousand ways to prevent them from the simple act of meditation. This is funny.

All I ask is that you begin with 5 minutes a day where you do nothing but observe Silence. Turn off your phone and put it in another room. Make some tea, this is the same thing as in tennis where before the serve, the player bounces the ball a few times. Making tea is preparing your mind and purifying. When I was 12 and doing Transcendental Meditation, we did twelve yoga postures and seven minutes of breathing exercises before meditating, so making tea is a lot easier. Whatever it is to tell yourself that you are going into a prayerful place and you will not be bringing the outer world and all its chaos with you. Wear loose clothing, and begin to breath deeply. Start your breathing awareness before you sit down to meditate. Just begin to take deeper breaths, very naturally. But deeper.

Then just meditate daily. You think you have no time to meditate, but after you do it, you realize you just created time. I like to keep a pen and paper around to record any ideas or thoughts that came as these are like paying an expensive mentor for advice, yet they come from your inner mentor.

53. BODY SCANNING MEDITATION

Make some tea. Sit down, relax and take a sip of tea. Smell the tea. Feel it on your tongue, in the back of your throat. Put the cup down. Now take your awareness slowly up and down your spine. Then bring your awareness to your head, the top of your head, down your spine and down each leg to the toes. Slowly bring your awareness up you ankle, calf, knees, legs, base of spine. Linger in each of the chakra areas, feeling the different sensations in each area, maybe visit your organs, and notice how the energy relaxes as you go there. You can notice the expanding everywhere you go, or allow

DREAM FULFILLMENT TOOLKIT

dilation like a camera lens opening. Just go open up.
Finish with being in your heart space and noticing what
you notice. Try and just be there. Be in your heart.
Notice beingness.

Take time to have a sip of tea and write any colors you
noticed, or energy, sounds, get comfy getting to know
your inner self. This is a fun introduction to meditation.
Being is having, this is a law or principle of abundance.
This is actually a very high havingness meditation and
puts you in touch will all sorts of goodies. Congratulate
yourself often for BEINGNESS. Good job!

54. SPIRITUAL HAVINGNESS

*Remember those moments of extreme joy, that one perfect
note, from that all is created.   ~Kevin Ryerson*

A sensitive person with low havingness is in a constant
state of lack. They may give to others and feel givers
high, but they themselves cannot receive. They don't
have the ability to receive and to own something simply
in order to have it for themselves. Instead, everything
they allow themselves to receive is because it will
somehow benefit someone other then themselves. They
feel a tremendous amount of guilt when it comes to

having something that is just their own, a secret jewel just for them, just because. In healing, we have to be able to HAVE and receive healing in order for us to heal. Can we have spiritual truth?

"Before you heal someone, ask him if he's willing to give up the things that make him sick." –Hippocrates

For so many of us, we practice giving on a daily basis — that is, giving to others. What we don't do is practice giving love, affection, or attention to ourselves. This often manifests as an underlying belief in their deserving to have or to receive.

There is a physical arena of havingess and a spiritual arena of havingness.

What if we were all allowed to have everything we wanted, as long as the desire was manifested in our hearts and fed by Source energy? Guess what, we do! Our deepest desires and fears are reflected to us in our reality. The spirit knows it can have whatever it needs to learn and grow, plus the things it wants to keep the body comfortable while achieving growth. But so often, our bodies and minds have been programmed into believing that we have to be deserving of something in order for us to have it.

How about the idea of growing through joy and wellbeing? There are beliefs inherent in our race consciousness claiming we only grow through pain. Pain is a great motivator, but must we have the concept of pain, or lack or poverty is a requirement of holiness?

The spirit world doesn't work that way. It is human to say that something is morally right or wrong, good or bad, or that someone is deserving or undeserving. The spirit world doesn't see good or bad, right or wrong, it just sees what is. I'm sure we can all think of someone who is a total schmuck who has everything they want. That person may have a sketchy moral character, but they also have high havingness.

Havingness = our ability to have.

Our level of havingness affects our health and healing, too. If you've been struggling with your health, take a moment to check in with yourself and notice how much you're able to let yourself have healing. Be honest with yourself.

How do we create havingness? Raising our havingness is a practice that involves understanding that we are inherently deserving of having the life and health that we desire and that when our health is off, it is our choice whether to stay a victim or take action. Taking action means more than going through the motions of healing — it means digging deep and noticing whether there are beliefs you have about yourself that need to change and then making a commitment to changing those beliefs— no matter how uncomfortable the process is. And, going to a doctor or specialist and taking right action if it is called for.

There is a spiritual tool for increasing havingness that's a bit more simple if you have a regular meditation practice. After grounding and calling back your energy, you can imagine a bubble out in front of you. In the bubble, see a gauge to appear with your level of havingness. Maybe 10 on top and 0 on the bottom. Notice the number. Now ground your gauge to the center of the planet and allow the grounding chord to release from the gauge any energy that's not allowing you to have what you want or need. See the energy move to the center of the planet. You may be able to identify it, but you don't have to. You may feel yourself lighten. What is happening is you are removing the energetic blueprint of lack. Can you allow yourself to energetically release nano particles of lack?

Watch your gauge, it may have moved upward. If not, take your (naughty) psychic finger and move it up to 100%. What happens is 100 percent means you are 100 percent in the heart of God. Spirit works immediately. Notice what happens.

Sounds easy, right? It is!

Havingness is a concept; it is the same as God presence or awareness of Source. As a spirit in a body, Beingness and Havingness are the same thing. Beingness is Havingness. When you are Being, that is you are consciously BEING you are Having at the highest level of your Self.

55. JOY OF BEING

Get in touch with your Joy of Being by meditating in Silence for a few minutes, and begin to notice your breath. Notice your animal-ness of your body. Your body strength, then notice your spiritual strength, notice there is a difference. Notice your body breath, the inner rise and fall of you belly as you breath, and tune into your joy of being. There are many other emotions going on. Surrender and only go to your joy of being. It is there. Just tune into your joy of living. Stay there for 20 minutes.

56. INFINITY

Chakras, and the meridian system are the nervous system of the soul. That energy is like a rainbow that extends into infinity or a hologram, by which we create our birth, events in our life, and since we are mortal, our return to spirit–having been energy all the time. This energy inside us is who we are all the time. Because we had a part in the creation of our body means we have the information on how to heal ourselves. Heal the spirit and the spirit will heal the body. This means becoming aware that spirit is a part of God, therefore perfect. It can only be what God is. If you have any other idea of who you are, change it to Truth. Faith in your perfection brings it forward in your consciousness. You are not broken in any way. If you perceive anything other than the perfection of your spirit, you are seeing though the body's awareness, which cannot see the perfection. Bodies die. Spirit is Eternal. If you have in you patterns, knowledge, light from the beginning of time, before the earth, how can you be anything other than perfection? You have to surrender a lot to come to this realization, but don't worry about the how and the why, just dwell in your perfection or will to.

There is no time or space as spirit therefore the most evolved state of the spirit, or Christ consciousness or Buddha consciousness exists as well as less evolved forms in you now. Your holiness is not out there in the future. In fact if you make statements such as, when I do a, b, and c then I can be happy, or holy, or whatever, you keep putting your awareness of your Divine Self out in the future – it will always be in a place you are not. It's all here now. Your true Self cannot be any other place then here and now. The miracle was not created for the already holy and perfect. It was created to get there. Grace happens in the midst of pain and turmoil, it is a God intervention. You do not have to do a thing to have grace. All you do is ask, or decree. It is all here now!

Making room for that which you cannot comprehend is all that is asked. There needs to be a clean place in your mind with nothing in it for God to show up in consciousness (God is already there, being everywhere all at once). You only need to surrender being right about things. The Course in Miracles asks, do you want to be right or happy? Next time you're struggling with an issue, see what happens when you give up being right about things.

As Jesus said in John 14:12 "Truly, truly, I say to you, the one who believes in me the works I do, shall he do also, and greater than these shall he do."

One can choose **enlightenment at any moment** by identifying with their immortal spirit in its highest state of evolution. Creative energy inside your creative inner self, your inner template is creating your own reality. We are Multi dimensional beings - we are already living in the fourth dimension as a society. Your Insights can apply to the here and now: Who am I, where am I going, how do I get there?

Ask who am I? Notice, who is watching you. Notice what

aspect of yourself is watching you.

Visualization is a meditation to see what is possible. It is much like imagination, where you deal in its realm and clarify what is possible. Then imagination, synchronicity and dharma begin to bring to you the different components of your vision and then you are manifesting a vision, and you are fulfilling the higher prophecy of the ability of being a visionary. Refine your inner talent, or dharma. When you practice, your work becomes a prayer, and you experience your own enlightenment.

Good news: it can be a hobby! Practicing your right work or your dharma, Synchronistic days begin to occur, and you're seeing how the universe really works. Your emotions, your energy template aligns with the practice of your enlightenment and joy comes to you with continuity like the river.

Remember those moments of extreme joy, that one perfect note, from that all is created.   John 4:8 "Whoever does not love does not know God, because God is love."

57. GOOD JOB

Habit of saying Good job, no matter what happens,

validate yourself. Are you still doing this?

You get to learn, mistakes are unmanifested wisdom, so learn! No matter what happens, or happened. Say good job and validate yourself!

58. MOCKUPS

A mock-up is a model, or prototype, of something that we want to create. This techniques involves visualizing, in your mind's eye, an mental image that contains what you desire to bring about. It's probably easier to start with your eyes closed. Remember, what we think has great creative power, and when we visualize our intention it becomes even more powerful.

Pretend that you are waving a giant bubble wand and have just made a very big, clear bubble. See it out in front of you. It can be as large as you'd like. In your bubble, begin to create a picture of what you want to have happen. It really is as simple as that. Be sure to take time to add to your vision as many details as possible of what you desire. The clearer we are about what we want, the more likely we are to get it!

When you have filled in as many details as you want, the next step is to let it go. As we let it go, we release our limited ideas of how things need to happen, and allow God, the universe, our own higher selves to do the work in creating our heart's desires. One way to release your mock-up and allow it to manifest is to simply watch the bubble float up until it's out of sight, to come to fruition in the perfect way. Or you could watch in your mind's eye as it pops, or anything else that occurs to you. Have fun with it!

One thing I like to do before I let go of my mock-up bubble is to connect it to God, and ask that anything standing between me and its creation be released and that it come under grace and abundance. In that way, I acknowledge the ability of the God within to create my life without limits. I affirm the truth.

This is fun stuff! And the hardest thing about it is believing that we can, and then remembering to do it. As we ask, we are answered. A mock-up bubble, as a tool for manifesting our intention, is a prayer.

A mockup is mental image of something your desire. You see this image, experience it. Ground off all the energy that says it's hard to receive, or can't have it. Ground it, connect it to God, and release it to God for it's highest expression in Grace to come to you at the perfect time. Some put this image in their gold sun, some in their grounding cords. Let go and go about your life.

59. CENTER OF HEAD

The center of your head is another term for neutrality. When we are neutral we are not swayed. It is a center of being and control place. If you are in the center of your head and you find someone, ask them what they want. Ask them to leave. If they don't leave then see them disappear, just tap them until they drop into vapor and leave. Remember, this is symbolic and these are only pictures, but they operate until you change the game. This is about dominion. You can rule your mind, your mental images- they do not rule you. There are rules about controlling your 3rd eye and no ones belongs there but you. If you see someone there, and they don't obey you, then you have the right to kick them out, just as you wouldn't allow a stranger into your house or even a friend to stay when you are ready to work.

Create a comfy chair right in the center of your head, own your center of your head. Between your ears, ground the center of your head and be in it. This is a safe place and the command center of your being. It is valuable because you can create in neutrality there. There is a reason your 6th chakra is your 3rd eye, and if this is full of light, you will be full of light.

The Lamp of the body.

For where your treasure is, there your heart will be also. Matthew 6:22-23 King James Version (KJV)
[22] The light of the body is the eye: if therefore thine eye be single, thy whole body shall be full of light.

[23] But if thine eye be evil, thy whole body shall be full of darkness. If therefore the light that is in thee be darkness, how great is that darkness!

60. AMUSEMENT

I've mentioned amusement, but it's worth mentioning again. If you are not amused, you are vulnerable because whatever has made you serious has control of your life. The Course in Miracles says the whole separation started when a soul forgot to laugh.

61. BODY OF GLASS

Body of glass is a good tool for your spiritual toolbox. It is the concept where by you exist as glass and allow energy, confusion, discord to flow right though you as light flows through glass. Nothing sticks but your good.

62. PROTECTION ROSE

A protection rose is a mental image of a rose that tells you how far out your aura is. If you keep your aura near around you, you are responsible for yourself. The more things, people you allow in your aura, the more you are responsible for because that is your personal space. It's like your home. If you allow people in your home, then they are in your space. You will be the effect of whatever they do because they are in your home. This is the concept. You can bring your energy to gold and everything will be neutralized to a high vibration. You can place a protection rose at the edge of your aura to tell you what you are allowing into your space. You can see the rose either brighten or wilt, and know you may need to replenish with gold suns, or just tune into Divine Harmony. I always ground my rose and connect it to God. This rose is God and only loving thoughts can come into my mind. Each time we create a protection rose it becomes more effective. So daily creation or hourly creation may be necessary depending on how much you are allowing in. You can place a grounded protection rose in front of your tv. So that energy is grounded and brought to God before it comes into your mind. You can place protection roses at your door, in front of your phone, car, meeting, relationship. Play with them. Notice what you notice.

63. MOCKUPS AGAIN

Michael Beckwith talks about the 4 stages of consciousness in his Visioning Book. Get this book! It's Awesome!

In the first stage, Victim Consciousness, you cannot have mockups, in the 2nd stage, this is where Mockups are created and manifested with ease. You are learning. Parking spaces are automatic, divine timing is normal. If you are suddenly not enjoying creating mockups, the next tool is havingness gauge. Create a mental image picture of a gauge and look at your havingness as a scale of 1-100. If its not at around 90 or higher, ground the gauge and release all the energy that is blocking your mockup. Flood the gauge with Gold God vibration. Notice how you feel. This gauge can be used for all sorts of things.

64. TRUTH OR LIE ROSE

Think of a situation in your life and reduce it to a yes or now. Do I or Don't I? Is this right for me?

In meditation, create a rose and think of a situation you know you like. See a rose for this. Notice the rose, how open the leaves, how healthy.

Create another rose

Think of a lie. Such as I have 3 ears. Notice the rose. Is it still healthy? What happens when there is a lie. What do you do energetically?

Practice this till you get a sense of what truth looks like and what a lie looks like.

Then take a subject that you really don't know the answer to, like it's time invest my time and energy for 8 weeks in this class about poetry right now. Look at your rose. Notice.

Then say, this is not the time to invest my time and energy in this 8 week poetry class. See what the rose does.

65. INNER VISION

Get quiet inside and relax. Do some body scanning and end up in the center of your head. Create a soft place for you to be there. Relax and notice your deep breath. See a gauge about 12 inches in front of your eyes. Notice where it is, and decide if low is on the bottom or which side – everyone sees the gauge in their own way, mine is vertical. Ground the gauge; connect to the Supreme Being, or God. Now, with your naughty psychic finger, if that gauge isn't at 100% raise it. Notice what happens to the gauge. You are in your havingness. Notice when you are in 100% havingness, there is very little you want. You just want to stay in the feeling. It is a feeling, a tone, a knowing of absolute joy, of the peace from beyond, and knowing of your eternal Self and that all of heaven is with you at all times. As the Course in Miracles says, you are not only in the Kingdom of Heaven; you ARE the kingdom of Heaven. You know if something will serve you it will be in your life, you forgive all things because you know in this state you never condemned. You are Grace itself.

This is a good meditation to start with at the beginning of your meditation and then you can have some quality time in your meditation. What I've learned is that you can sit for hours staring at your belly button and end up frustrated in meditation. The sooner you going into the Presence of God in your awareness, the more amazing your meditation will be.

66. DEEP THOUGTHS

"The deeper you go, the more power is available to change things. The easiest way to change anything is to first go to the subtlest level of it, which is awareness. Still silence is the beginning of creativity. Once an event starts to vibrate, it has already begun to enter the visible world. Creation proceeds by quantum leaps. The beginning of an event is simultaneously its ending. The two co-arise in the domain of silent awareness. Events unfold in time but are born outside of time. The easiest way to create is in the evolutionary direction. Since possibilities are infinite, evolution never ends. The universe corresponds to the nervous system that is looking at it." - Depak Chopra

67. DIVINE DANCE

Whatsoever ye shall do, do it heartily, as to the Lord, and not unto (people). ~ Colossians 3:23

Dance with your Divine Self, feel her animate your body as you dance, now dance with her, imagine her leading you. Feel how that feels, notice your joy of being.

Experiential Yes!

Play with this such as.. Every time you climb stairs, (or walk down a certain hall) think of victory, maybe put your arms up in a V. Imagine cheering, imagine winning, success, not so much a thing, just as the emotion of success, of victory, of YES!

68. MOBILITY

Mobility is not only about destination. The dictionary says it's: the ability to move or be moved freely and easily, or it is the ability to move between different levels in society or employment. I'm talking about spiritual mobility.

Think of your ability to go where you need to go, or your ability to go where you want to go physically, mentally or emotionally. Can you move out of an emotion? Sometimes we are in the grip of an emotion, even a victim of our emotions. I would gladly be a victim of joy! But I'm talking about being a victim of lower unhealthy emotions. Jealousy, competition, anger, hate, the world is against me. Did you know that when you are angry, you send anger out in your world and create more situations that make you angry? Sometimes when a situation happens that creates anger in us, it can create a downward spiral. Depression can do the same.

The second you feel hatred you have to stop or it can do damage. Realize you always have a choice – choose again with Love.

69. LAUGH JAR

What if you trained yourself to laugh every time something that seemed bad happened? An inner sense of amusement at earth school. It sounds sick and demented, but raising your energy works. It is the low vibration that caused the trouble to manifest in the physical world in the first place. If you stay in low energy, you can create a chain reaction of horrible events. It is an act of rebellion to laugh in the face of trouble. I mean an inner amusement.

Sometimes people want to control you with anger. If you notice when you laugh at someone who is angry with you it sometimes makes them angrier? That is when you know their anger is control device. You have to laugh on the inside, because controllers who use anger are intent on ruining your good mood, and sometimes they will do whatever it takes to bring you down. This is subtle, they do it unconsciously, and it is a call for love, (because they are an aspect of ourselves – we are doing to ourselves) but it's hard to be compassionate when someone is spewing volcanic molten hate at you. Laughing at them, is taking a step back, and is a form of mobility, and actually puts you in a place where you can see the bigger picture, you cannot see the bigger picture if you are bathed in their searing violence of anger. If you do not want to be the effect of the anger, then you can do something about the root cause. In this case, a sudden outburst of anger, you need its opposite, a sudden outburst of laugher. But don't show it, just step back in your mind, and do what it takes, the best thing is to remember what makes you belly laugh. Silently distance yourself and laugh on the inside.

Can you keep a jar of things that make you laugh, or belly laugh? These are powerful and we can have them around incase we loose it.

Don't just take my word for it:

[Humanity] has unquestionably one really effective weapon—laughter. Power, money, persuasion, supplication, persecution—these can lift at a colossal humbug—push it a little—weaken it a little, century by century, but only laughter can blow it to rags and atoms at a blast. Against the assault of laughter nothing can stand. ~ Mark Twain

> A good laugh heals a lot of hurts. ~ Madeleine L'Engle

Always laugh when you can. It is cheap medicine. ~ Lord Byron

An optimist laughs to forget; a pessimist forgets to laugh. ~ Tom Nansbury

God has a smile on His face. ~ Psalm 42:5

Grim care, moroseness, and anxiety—all this rust of life ought to be scoured off by the oil of mirth. Mirth is God's medicine. ~ Henry Ward Beecher

He deserves Paradise who makes his companions laugh. ~ Koran

He that is of a merry heart has a continual feast. ~ Proverbs 15:15

I commend mirth. — Ecclesiastes 8:15

Each of us has a spark of life inside us, and our highest endeavor ought to be to set off that spark in one another. ~ Kenny Ausubel

Earth laughs in flowers. ~ Ralph Waldo Emerson

Even the gods love jokes ~ Plato

As soap is to the body, so laughter is to the soul. ~ A Jewish Proverb

As soon as you have made a thought, laugh at it.

~ Lao Tsu

If you become silent after your laughter, one day you will hear God also laughing, you will hear the whole existence laughing — trees and stones and stars with you. ~ Osho

In life, there are belly laugh times, when you laughed so hard your sides hurt, remember those, write them down, and have an image, just a flash. When we collect mental images that make us laugh, and use them as a place to put our mind when we lose our joy of being we make it easier. When we do this we are mobile. We have choice. We are taking charge of things that bring our energy way up. This is actually good for the whole planet because we are energy raising. When we decide not to contribute to someone's anger, or sadness, or grief, we are mobile. If we sink our energy down and don't understand that we went there and we can go somewhere else, then we are less mobile. A Course in Miracles says, choose again, with love.

70. SYMPATHY

If someone (appears to be) sick and you go into sympathy with the illness, you are telling them on subtle levels that the illness is a reality and they are not a capable spirit, or a perfect and holy child of God and therefore sickness is impossible. Spirits can't get sick. We are spirits in bodies. When we identify as spirit, and more powerfully, a spirit bound in thought to the Divine, we are stating our essential truth of being as a creation of the divine and therefore spiritually perfect in all ways.

Sickness is a mistaken belief that may be taking form and becoming a fact, but we can unbelieve it, and turn to the essential eternal God Truth of someone, and start believing from there. You can remember for them, who they are.

We can wake up that Glory inside the person, that angel aspect of that person, and call them to arise boldly and shout their hallelujah sound that re-patterns their health into wholeness that was always there. This may take time in the world (or be instant), but energetically it is done and finished. God inside them doeth the works.

"Spring up, O well! All of you sing to it." – Numbers 21:17

You can have sympathy with the person, but never with the illness. This is another form of mobility. Can you step back from someone's belief that they are sick? (It is impossible that anyone be sick, as they are a perfect holy child of God, the form of sickness is an untrue illusion). This is a form of mobility, of choosing to see the truth

God created instead of being an effect of the world of form.

Those with pain are pulled whereas those with divine vision are pushed.

71. VIBRATION

Here is a scale with a range of emotions with energy vibrations. You will notice that Enthusiasm and Joy are at the top, being the lightest vibration and boredom and death are on the bottom of the scale being heavier energies.

Joy, Appreciation, Empowered, Freedom

Passion

Enthusiasm, Eagerness, Happiness

Positive Expectation, Belief

Optimism

Hopefulness

Contentment

Boredom, Pessimism

Frustration, Irritation, Impatience

Overwhelmed

Disappointment

Doubt, Worry, Blame

Discouragement

Anger

Revenge

Hatred, Rage

Jealousy

Insecurity, Guilt, Unworthiness

Fear, Grief, Depression, Despair, Powerlessness

The word emotion is e motion. Motion. The higher the motion the higher the well being and joy. The lower the motion the more disappointment can take over.

I've heard of top therapists with high client success rates who will not take clients that don't do intensive exercise at least three times a week. Part of their success is that they know exercise does half their therapy work. Just moving your body puts you in a higher energy state. The benefits of exercise are enumerable on many levels.

When you are mobile, you are able to move yourself into any vibration of your choice. Amusement is a very high vibration and is close to enthusiasm. The higher vibrations are very creative and appear radiant.

When you are in a low vibration it is easy to be stuck. You can be stuck on a past life picture, on an issue, or illness, and when you are in that energy, you can absolutely forget about the your higher energies. The lower energies take a thousand times more energy to create in, and those who forgot that they could change anytime like to have company in the mud pit. One way to get some separation from these emotions is humor. Humor raises your energy and it is a powerful healing tool. When you use humor as a tool, you are actively raising the energy vibration for everyone. If you cannot find humor, you use fake humor, ha, ha, ha. Say, ha, ha, ha in a bored voice. An Opera laugh? Woody Woodpecker laugh? Can you say, ha, ha, ha in a bored voice? Keep saying ha, ha, ha until something shifts and it will. Fake amusement is a tool to use when you are stuck.

Just like laughing at something like the news. Only a callous person would laugh at the misfortune of others, but I'm not saying that at all. Repeat, this is not about laughing at the misfortune of others. This is about removing yourself mentally from problems and negativity, so you can be a more effective healing agent.

You can be compassionate for the person but not the illness, sickness, or problem. If you are an uncontrolled healer, you will give more reality to the problems, sickness and loss of inspiration, and reaffirm that the person has no ability to change. Amusement is about making you a more effective healer, because you will have mobility and choice in what you choose to heal – are you reinforcing the problem or its solution?

Alas, some people who are in a low vibration and in their victimhood have no desire to change. They are getting something out of being a victim. They don't want to change, and no amount of prayer, or healing is going to move them until they decide. **Remember Hippocrates who said, before you decide to heal a person ask him if he's willing to give up what's making him sick**.

This is another occasion to say, ha, ha, ha. When you give them your very best, and are keeping your energy very high so you can share your goodness, and they don't want any of it, you need to laugh. They want to sit there and complain, this is an occasion to laugh at taking yourself too seriously. This is a subtle awareness, and it cuts through problem thinking.

Remember the Emotion Scale? When we are in the body's emotions the opposite emotion will eventually balance out. If you spend years in grief, later happiness will balance out. *Joy is an emotion that has no opposite and it is different than happiness.* **Joy and enthusiasm**

have at their root, an eternal quality that has no opposite. Entheos means in god. Happiness for a thing can be taken away if that thing leaves. Or, you can begin to take it for granted and that happiness becomes flat.

Advertising and our consuming culture leads us by the nose with the idea that once we get something we will be happy, or have status, or have arrived. Sleeping pills don't solve the problem if they need more exercise. Advertising says, take this drug and you will be just fine. You need a certain amount of money, your mother back, a partner that has certain qualities, and then happiness will be achieved. The point I'm making is that when happiness is attributed to getting something (getting is a condition), it sets up its opposite. The beginning of something has its end as well; there is no time on an energy level. If you take time out of the equation, and just look at the intention; if I get A, then B will happen.

What if B will happen, or B is happening and this is what it feels like. (Feel what it feels like to have achieved B. The subconscious is a great creator; it believes anything you tell it. I'm rich! Oh, I'm rich I'm rich! Living in this, somewhere, lurking in the shadows is the opposite thought. No you're not; it's not possible, bla, bla, bla. Or it will be difficult; of there are too many walls to achievement.

Lack is there, if only in the group consciousness of society, so here comes the denial. There is no opposite of God; therefore there is nothing that can prevent this if it is

God's will. I will to have all that God wills for me.

72. CHARMED LIFE

"Having lots of money while not having inner peace is
like dying of thirst while bathing in the ocean."
~Paramahansa Yogananda

I have a billionaire acquaintance, who has always had a
charmed life. Well that is what it seemed like. Actually,
when you look under the surface, there are some
heartbreaking trials in that family. Some people who have
a huge amount of money are not in control, their money
controls them and their entitlement sets up all sorts of
dilemmas. For some people, a lot of money is not their
dharma. An example of this is someone who thinks
having a swimming pool will make them happy, they
manifest it and now have to take care of that pool. It's a
lot of work, they now have to work more hours to keep
the pool working. For others, the pool is no work at all.
An inner sensing of what is right and wrong for you,
being connected to your inner guidance benefits
everyone. And sometimes those who are the most wealthy
spiritually have very little money, yet they live in a state
of joy, have loving friendships with those who share their

passion and joy, enjoy their food, are peaceful, feel abundantly provided for. The are WELLthy. They are well. Wealth is an idea of ease. If you can vibrate in the base vibration of what you think wealth will give you, the things that support that will show up in your life. You will attract what you are. This is like putting the cart before the horse. Living in a joyful state of meditation, things, people, situations come before you ask — in the vibration of joy.

73. MANIFESTING

Think of something you want. A physical object. What are the good things this will give you? For example, if you want a bike. The base vibration of having a bike might be, freedom, mobility, joy, and adventure.

Think of the effects you will enjoy as you are doing this thing.

Can you go into the feeling tone, the color?

Can you go into the very essence of the good? Sit in that essence. Really bath in it. Remind yourself to be in this good, to have your beingness your vibration in the good you will have in the future, if you see it, and then hold that picture, but the picture doesn't matter, the feeling of good matters. This attracts many things to you that bring you that essence.

Note: If you have anxiety, or are forcing, stop and bath in God essence. Allow yourself to be surrounded by angels and heal and then stop. If you ever go chasing after something you want and feel anxiety, you must stop and sink into your heart.

74. MANIFESTING GOD

When we vibrate in the good, or God, then the universe can give us better than we asked for because we are letting go of the how and they why. We have to remember if we have to micromanage God, our idea of God is really limited. If God created everything, then God knows the secret longings of our heart, what is good for us, and where our unending joy is. When we can give up and trust, the universe flows with us and coincidences show up and we know the universe wants us to have more joy than we can imagine. God can only give us what we can allow. As we change in consciousness, we have more miracles in our life. We are guided by an internal knowing. When we stop trying to get things and learn that by giving we receive, that teaching is learning that we can only have a miracle by giving it away, we learn that only by wanting to be *truly* helpful, true helpfulness can show up in our life. Giving of Divine Gifts becomes joyful; *Spirits know* that giving is receiving, so you are receiving Divine Gifts as you give them away.

For some, the right amount of money causes them to evolve. They are doing what they came here to do. We are here to bring Heaven to earth. Even if we are born in terror, and horrible things happen to us, we are still here to transcend and help others. We are here to overcome problems and know and demonstrate that **a problem is an opportunity for spiritual magnificence.** We are here to demonstrate we are under no laws but Gods. We are not the effect, we are Source! Or Source expresses through us in our actions, thoughts, willingness and love.

Manifestors eventually learn that there are consequences to having things, or situations that are not completely under Gods Guidance and Will. Manifestors start out manifesting wonderful things and learn how our thoughts really are creating our reality, and sooner or later we will have to let go of our will, and will learn Joy is in a greater Will and it operates on a grand scale. It's a wonderful place. Just as the lower chakras are duality and involve effort because they are body chakra's, Channel consciousness is spiritual and involves no effort at all. It is an idea, it is Mind. This is a form of mobility.

The ability to have what God wills for you is a form of mobility. It is moving from what you think you want, taking a break, going within and asking for inner direction.

Going within is like letting go, of surrendering everything, every thing we are holding onto we drop, all the lists, drop away, all the planning is let go of and unravels. We stand naked, with nothing in our hands, before our Source, no goals except surrender, and notice the soft inner self breathing. We have no problems we are chewing on because we have no gods before God. And in our holy breath and silence, we wait with no thoughts, only an intense listening, only a vacant place so our divine Guidance can be heard in the divine language of love. It comes in a flash, so if you are listening to your inner chatter, it will be missed. This is a holy moment of silence and guidance.

You might have high mobility in one area, but not in another. Some people have very high physical mobility, but they can't bring their joy with them, they travel to exotic destinations, but there is always a series of problems, or anxiety. Some people never leave their home, and then they CAN move about in their consciousness with ease, or they cannot, or fall somewhere in-between. The idea of mobility that I'm describing is about energy and willingness and mental abilities that animate mobility.

75. RAISE YOUR HAVINGNESS

You have a higher mobility. You may even want to look at your gauge of havingness for mobility. Clear it out and connect it to God or the Supreme Being, or Divine Love. Notice what happens.

This is a concept I will come back to again and again, the substance behind objects. When you have your highest mobility going on, you arc lcd to places where you need to be that are always joyful or healing. You may be on the bumpiest, economy flight, but surrounded by your soul mates, maybe helping someone or deeply connected to fellow traveler soul guide who has a message for you. We go into the problem and find the most odious person whom we resisted the most is in fact our savior.

You may even be led to the grocery story down the street, but something will happen. When we decide we want to be truly helpful, we allow ourselves to be guided. There will be a soul connection and you will feel the warmth of healing as you offer it. Healing is always for ourselves. We give what we want to receive, we receive what we give. When you offer your Self to be a healing agent in the world, that generosity is aimed right back to you and will come in unexpected ways. When you come from your spirit, and offer love, it returns amplified. When you give from lack, or with a string attached, then lack is what you receive. When you offer true forgiveness you receive it for yourself. If you offer one-sided forgiveness, you receive it back, maybe not from the same person. You know the deep healing will show up when you want only that in all your communications.

76. DECLARING IN FAITH

I remember when I first started light working, and one of the affirmations was "all relationships are healing relationships'. I laughed and really wondered if that could ever be true. Some relationships were so fraught with games that it was ridiculous to think they could ever change. Years later, I now believe and see the effects of how I feel when I decide that my communications are laced with Gods love. My faith is substance and my conviction is law.

All communications are healing ones.

This changes how I experience a communication. I must say that sometimes my faith is all I have in some communications, and my fears come up and really screw up some relationships, and then I can go back into affirming, declaring and know, sooner or later the love will show up, and in that declaration, on an energy level, it is accomplished. It will show up in time, and I will take steps, by listening to my inner guidance on what is right. What I don't quite yet understand is that I am guided sometimes to really push back. To defend myself, or to yell at someone until they understand that I am upset or need space. I mean really unload. What I find is that I'm honoring myself, even though I've made an unfriendly environment for another person in my life and they will leave. We both make room for someone more attuned to our growth areas or redefine a more respectful relationship.

I say this because we think things will make us happy, or have our good in some way, or a destination, or a person, or a communication, like a partner, when I have this amount of friends, a partner, a home in a certain style, then I will be happy and I can relax. There are a few problems here:

1. Specific things can be taken away. Or may not come exactly as you want, and so they won't have the charge. This sets up a mind game. I can't have… I never get…

2. When you have the inner energy or movement of, when I get Z (therefore) I will feel A. Even the math doesn't work. But that is how our society with all the advertisements, work on our subconscious. Every commercial you have ever

watched is still programming your subconscious (unless you actively clear it out). Once you buy our product, you will have status, acceptance, power, wealth, love, happiness. So we think when we get these things it works, but that is just the advertising story. When you get a sense of your inner power, outer things no longer have sway over you and cause you to go chasing rainbows.

3. It's all here now. When you have an inner feeling of success, or happiness, joy, mobility (being at the right place at the right time), the outer form that matches will show up better than your expectations.

4. Faith in yourself is what begins to start this action. Instead of having faith once you receive your object, you have faith that it is already accomplished, and that God takes the last step and you are in the feeling of accomplished good. When you start seeing how this works then you begin to see how this concept can be applied to larger aspects of reality and creation and you can shift situations, by your own inner shift.

"If you are in balance you can turn poison into nectar. If you are out of balance you will turn nectar into poison."
~Deepak Chopra

Go way out. Think beyond your present dreams and aspirations to the dreams you'll have once the former dreams are realized. And when you can clearly imagine who confident you'll walk and proud you will feel, start walking and feeling that way today. -The Universe

77. INNER MYSTERY

To begin getting in touch with the inner mystery, consciously dance with your Divine Self. You can also imagine you are dancing with your favorite Deity, saint or Source Itself. When you do this, even for a second, it is joyful. No one needs to know and you are doing this privately. This is a meditation space. It's actually good to dance for a minute or so every hour, even if when you are walking down the hall, you embody your body, and feel your Divine Self. You will move in a whole new way. Sense your heart self, I know how I do it, and you have your own way that no one can define for you. It is known by your conscious awareness and no one can do it for you.

This is bringing your meditation practice right into life. Meditating in the same chair is good for knowing your inner self, and now we are bringing that right into your life.

The Course in Miracle exercises do reprogram your whole mind, and they ask that you do the affirmations in every area of your day, and life. Not in the same place, so that is why the dancing and moving with spiritual awareness.

78. MOBILITY GUAGE new thing

Make a gauge for your mobility, ground it, and ground yourself. Begin to release anything that you are ready to release. Just allow it to go down your grounding, or leave. (If it's not God, it's not real. All unreality goes back into the nothingness from which it came.) If it's grounding out, imagine the center of the earth recycling it. If it's leaving your space, then imagine as it is not a part of God, it has no existence. It goes back into the nothingness from which it came. If all is God, and God is Good, then everything else is an illusion. You want only what God wants for you. There is one will and it's Gods Will. Experience that!

This idea takes your right out of your duality and into your eternal reality. When you are at the point in your consciousness when you want only what God wants for you, then you are always at the right place and the right time, because you become aware that your whole existence revolves around your consciousness. If you start giving up what you can get and go into what you can give, you will be truly helpful, this puts you on a joyful trajectory. You receive things before you want them because you are in alignment with a higher flow.

79. VICTIM CONSCIOUSNESS

This is simplistic but it helps us see that we have choices and where our edge of learning is. You can also see where someone is by what they want to create in the VBCS- the higher the evolution the more they want God qualities such as love, joy, life, peace, serenity, bliss, mainly because these vibrations attract everything that brings them these qualities. For example, instead of envisioning the Best Case Scenario for a bike, they will VBCS vision for freedom, joy and mobility (or whatever inner feelings they think having a bike will give them). Then everything that brings joy and mobility is attracted in grace.

Someone in Victim consciousness will not understand this. Also.. we all go from one stage of consciousness to another. For some there may be a level where they exist most of the time.

The first level is Victim- the world is doing it to you. If

you are vibrating in victim consciousness and plan to stay there, you will hate this book. You would have not read this far. If you are ready to move up you will love this book.

80. MANIFESTOR CONSCIOUSNESS

The second level is Manifestor- You become aware of how thought attracts things, parking places are pretty easy to manifest, as well as situations, things. This is one is a blast as you understand there is a co-operative spiritual plane that loves to give to you and with a joyful sense of humor. **This is the honeymoon of spiritual learning and it can go on for years.** Until you are ready to spiritually evolve and then it *seems to backfire*—you are wanting to understand the difference between ego desires and deeper spiritual yearning. As this becomes apparent your life might break down a little. It is the cocoon stage of a butterfly. If you refuse to learn it can become the dark night of the soul.

This sucks as a spiritual coach to see people here.. sometimes its more kind to let them go hard and fast to get it over with sooner. You can talk all you want.. you cannot learn for them.

81. CHANNEL CONSCIOUSNESS

The third level is Channel consciousness. This is where you live in the idea of wanting only God's Will and releasing your own will because there are so many loving coincidences that occur when you release your will. Miracles happen almost every day. You notice that the universe corresponds to your nervous system. You can almost seem to calm noise by meditating. Deepak Chopra makes great sense and you crave similar books. Meditation is salve.

82. CHRIST CONSCIOUSNESS

The 4th level is Christ Consciousness where you can be a Krishna, or Buddha. It is rare yet, every single person alive can have flashes of this at any time. Just saying, Greater works than these Ye Shall Do is every persons inheritance.

I've met people who must have been in the 4th level of

consciousness and seemed to have no idea or care that they were offering so much peace—their presence was so life giving! We will know you by your Works!

You do not need to say a thing, have a title, a prestigious job to do amazing energy work. You do not need to announce a thing to the world, you can get more accomplished if you do the energy work suggested here in silence.

We move from these levels of consciousness all the time, and hover around one level or a few. This ability to move into consciousness is mobility as well.

83. THE LORD'S PRAYER

IS AN AFFIRMATIVE PRAYER, IT IS a mini church service, it is powerful VBCS visioning:

1 A. Just like, *Our Father Who art in Heaven, hallowed be Thy Name.* We are invoking The Highest Creative Aspect in our entire Universe. We are declaring there is a power in the universe, which is much greater than we are. **When we ask, what is Gods Very Best Case Scenario for me,** we are invoking just like *Our Father Who Art in Heaven....Thy Kingdom come Thy Will be Done.*

When we create with *our will,* we are creating from our earthbound self, and its laws, and are not using the unlimited laws of the Divine. We want Divine will and its unlimited laws. We are **passive** and let go completely and deeply pay attention in the stillness. Our mind is a calm lake reflecting the light of the sun. (Matthew 6:22 If thine eye be single, the whole body will be filled with light.) Light is understanding.

2. A. *Forgive us our trespasses as we forgive those who trespass against us.* **What must I give up? What must I let go of?** Letting go of the idea that something is against us. Nothing is against us. If there is it *is in our mind* and we ask for a healing of letting go of anything which prevents our divine self in our mind. We ask God to heal our mind. **God, give For Me your wisdom, truth** instead of what ever I made up about life. Letting Go is asking God to step in. Give for us Your Truth *and Truth's laws.*

C. *Lead us not into temptation, and deliver us from evil.* Turn away from the idea that something is against us or a separate power, and allow any illusion that is ready to go, to be healed. Allow Divine truth to dissolve any sense of separation or pain to be released into the nothingness that it is.

3 and 4. *Give us this Day, our Daily Bread.* Bread means substance. Give us our Divine Substance; feed our soul your Life, Joy and Strength so we may do what is ours to

do with great Spiritual Style and the sparkle of abundance. What is Gods Divine Substance for me on this issue I'm asking about.

a. When you see, or intuit, sense, hear…or however you hear the Lord, you have a lot of Spiritual Support, and backing because you are in alignment with the order of the Universe. (What looks like a giant unsolvable mess in your life is nothingness to the Lord to Whom only creations of love are real.) This awareness is great when you get a tall order from God and can't believe that you are asked to do something that you can't quite wrap your mind around. This can be as simple as sensing a great peace in a situation you previously imagined to be horrific. You will have the peace. This is a miracle. It is shared.

4. *For Thine is the Kingdom and the power and the glory for ever and ever.* Celebrate! The Divine VERY BEST CASE SCENARIO for our issue is created and known (God makes a way when there is no way) in alignment with the higher order of the universe, and therefore, win/win/win.

Be grateful! This is a holy assignment and everything needed for its perfect execution is already given. We are bringing Heaven to earth. We are to rest in God and allow God to work through us. This is not to say we will sit around and do nothing. **Au contraire!**

We will listen within, to feel into what is right and wrong for us, but will sense the rightness and be inspired to work through any difficulty. The Accomplishment is done! It will show up in time. We will check in intuition and do as we are guided.

84. CIRCULATE ENERGY

"The Holy Spirit now works with irresistible goodness through me."

There are many ways to manifest; each breath can be manifesting abundance to a grateful person.

When I breathe in, Existence pours Its Love into me.
When I breathe out, I pour Love into my existence.

Breathe into God, and breath out God into your life. Have that intention and do a yoga inhale of deeply dragging in like you're inhaling holy smoke, but instead you are inhaling God or Gods love, light, and experience your life force increasing.

Chi, or Universal Life Force is increased by deep breathing and its free!

85. ALREADY THERE THANKYOU!

Think of something you want but you don't have it. Let that thing come to mind. Think of someone who has what you want. Either love, money, travel, a great career. Think of that person who has the thing you want.

If you can get this far then you already have it. You cannot imagine what you do not already have. If you could see it in someone, you can have it. It's like intuitive reading – you can't see what you are not. You only see through your own pictures.

So if this person has the thing you want, to bring its vibration into your field in a state of havingness, be grateful that this person already has the thing you want. Feel yourself overjoyed that they have it. The more you can be truly happy for someone's wealth, happiness, love because what God gives to others, God gives to me. If you feel envy or jealousy or competition then you push away God.

So then, know what God gives to others, God gives to me. There is no lack in God, so there is no lack other than in my mind. There is no lack in my mind, if I chose so. I chose abundance.

Now, turn to God. Go within, and look up. Look in your heart, look into the heart of God however you do.

Download God, or drink in God, or be illuminated by God, be fed, nourished by your Source. This God is ALREADY THERE; we are removing the blocks to loves presence by looking straight at the Presence. Just be in it for as long as you like and expand.

86. TITHING

Money represents a note of promise of energy that will be delivered – it is a promise of circulation. The circulation of energy money is not material, but people tend to see money as a material concept. A finite oblong piece of paper that you can easily tear up is a limited idea, and when we look at the physical aspect of money we don't see that what backs the money, what makes its value is the circulation which is unlimited. Se we may hoard, or hold our money in a limiting, not-enough sort of consciousness, and then not keep it circulating to the things that bring us life. The circulation of money in your life represents the circulation of your own energy. If you think of money like it is God.. you can't tie up God, no way, but you can really hurt yourself if you believe your Creator is mean and punishing or limiting.

When we limit our ideas around money we can keep the energy of money from circulating, and it can back up and stagnate and then it really is the root of evil because we blocked ourselves.

What does spiritual abundance have to do with money?

87. DESPENSER OF DIVINE GIFTS

The word Human in Sanskrit is manu or Brahma or dispenser of divine gifts.

Human means dispenser of divine gifts!

You can't be a Divine Dispenser if you think you are here to take; here to be entitled and consume, complain, dwell in low energy, refusing to look at your answered prayer, and creating a welcome environment for your answered prayer, and taking a step a day towards your answered prayer.

Joy is not something the world can take away. It is an activity of your awareness; joy can be in your awareness whether things are going well or not. The awareness of abundance can be in your awareness and practice even though it is not yet manifested. Our minds are pure potential, it is how we use them that determines our state of being.

Money is only the finite piece of paper, the real Medium

of exchange is infinite, and it is abundant as water in the ocean. It is how we use it that determines the flow.

"I open all channels of good towards me. All channels of money that are for my good now flow to me."

The promise, Gods Word is eternal, we are like the paper square of money, our body is, but our mind is an eternal temple of a living God. WE are receptors and communicators of unlimited Good!

Seeing money as only the paper and therefore limited aspect is the same concept of seeing yourself as only a body, and therefore only under the laws of this earth and therefor doomed, because you will die one day, or the money will be spent and then it's gone. Your real self is unbound by time and the limits of this world. Your true Self is unlimited joy, eternal peace, and knows what hallelujah means in ways you cannot wrap your mind around.

Abundance is like how God sees you, an eternal wellspring of all life. The paper aspect of money is a great way to see your body. Do you hoard and withhold love because you think if you give it, there will a lack in you? Or do you understand that the more you give love, the more receive it. The more you forgive the more you receive forgiveness. That when you withhold it is only from yourself.

88. ABUNDANCE PRAYER

From The Light of God that We Are.

From The Love of God that We Are.

From The Power of God that We Are.

From The Heart of God that We Are.

Lets Decree-

We dwell in the midst of Infinite Abundance. The Abundance of God is our Infinite Source.

The River of Life never stops flowing. It flows through us into lavish expression. Good comes to us through unexpected avenues and God works in a myriad of ways to bless us.

We now open our minds to receive our good. Nothing is too good to be true. Nothing is too wonderful to have happen. With God as our Source, Nothing amazes us.

We are not burdened by thoughts of past or future. One is gone. The other is yet to come.

By the power of our belief, coupled with our purposeful fearless actions and our deep rapport with God, our future is created and our abundance made manifest.

We ask and accept that We are lifted in this and every moment into Higher Truth. Our minds are quiet.

From this day forward We give freely and fearlessly into life and Life gives back to us with magnificent increase. Blessings come in expected and unexpected ways. God provides for us in wondrous ways for the work that we do.

I AM indeed grateful.

89. WE ALREADY HAVE

So, if we understand that the real money is like faith- the more you use faith, the more it creates wonderful things. Money is a promise, the good has already been received, (the bank is full of gold to back the money, so it can circulate and endlessly bring good to everyone) the next thing we want to know is how do we open up those channels, so it can flow to us.

When you give from an idea abundance, you create more flow. When you give money to the things, people and events that animate your soul, then you tell the universe to give you more things that animate your soul. Also, when you save money by paying yourself first, you are telling the universe that you have so much abundance, that you can save some, *and* you can tithe to that which feeds your soul. This is a declaration that you HAVE. If you did not have, you couldn't give to yourself or others.

The other side of this is always telling everyone how you don't have enough, can't do 'a, b or c' because you don't have enough money. When someone tells you of their fabulous new home, or trip, or kids made it to good college, and you either burn, or make some comment that comes out sarcastic, you are making a declaration to the universe on what it should do. Saying you don't have enough money to do something is saying it, therefore creating more of that. If you change your language to something that affirms you have plenty, and it feels good and right, start using those words, so you can tell the universe that all is well.

Like, I'm thrilled that you have a fabulous new house, and then you think, what God does for others, God does for me. Be thrilled for their new whatever, and know that you can have the same or better.

When others prosper, I prosper

When I prosper, others prosper

See how that unlocks the little fences in your mind?

Say something like.. 'Next year, who knows, I might be able to join you on a trip, (big smile upwards) or who knows what good might happen and my kid lands in a great college.' Find a way to say things that are telegraphing to the universe that you are ready for more flows of money or good to come your way. Words are powerful!

Another demonstration of havingness is to give to those who are in need, for example to a person who is about to get a new home (not homeless), or to a charity. Better yet, volunteer at a charity. This is a loud and clear statement to the universe that you have. You can only give what you have, and you are so overflowing, you can give in joy to others. You tell your subconscious, and the Universe that you have. Remember the Spiritual law: Those who have, can have more.

If you feel that you lack, or give with idea of getting something in return, or it hurts to give because you don't feel you have enough, or you give or pay in anger, you signal to the universe to demonstrate lack.

Envelopes of bills represent things already received – you already received the new espresso maker, the bill is only a reminder that energy flowed. Do not curse your bills, feel guilty at your debt, or curse money hungry corporations! Instead, give thanks that energy and good flowed to me before you had to do anything.

God has already given us the whole kingdom, it is exists in our minds in the now. When we are grateful for it, it comes into experience. Remember the Lord's Prayer?? *Thy Kingdom come, they will be done, on earth as it is in heaven.*

We already have ALL, it already happened; just like

when you buy things and then the bill comes.

90. NOTICE AND PRAISE THE FLOW!

God has already given me the whole kingdom; it's my job to notice heaven on earth by bringing heaven forward in my mind.

When I pay I become thankful and grateful that I get to return the favor of flow, but I am so abundant, I am going to increase the flow of good outward – I wish 10 times back to those who trusted me and sent me a bill. When you pay a bill, send an idea that you wish 10 times back to whomever sent you the bill. Be faith in practice! This is a strong abundance law! Give in joy! Wish others well for fun of it! You prime the pump when you do.

We aren't looking for the returned favor here. That is a string. No string. When you meditate in the joy of God, you are not looking for something back, you are being in Joy. You already have the whole kingdom.

91. PRAISING BILLIONAIRES

This might be offensive, but do you praise people who have money? You know how the 1% who is responsible for all the evil in the world? Well, if you are blaming the 1% you are repelling abundance. Actually if you are blaming anything or anyone you are repelling your divine inheritance.

Billionaires and politicians are holy children of God as well as you. Do you silently despise all rich politicians? If you do, then you repel abundance. You say to your unconscious that you will hate yourself when you become rich, or people will hate you. Remember that those who are rich can give more to charity. If you were a billionaire what would you do?

Just for the fun of it…Wear an aura of wealth, and allow the idea that you can have a million extra dollars going to nothing but activities that bring your joy of being to the front of your existence. This is not to say your joy of being isn't at the ocean, or on a hike in the mountains and that is free, this isn't the point of the exercise. It is to wear large amounts of money and pretend like you have 130,000.00 in the bank that is yours. How does that feel to have free extra money? Is that comfortable?

How about a million dollars just for your play and joy? Pretend you have all that money and you can do anything in the world with it. It's yours, tax-free. What does this feel like? Wear this aura, this idea.

Now, pretend you have thirty million in the bank. Notice what happens. Pretend you can give most of it to charities and helping others. Feel that.

Go to a place, a hotel, a restaurant, a club for the very, very wealthy, or Tiffany's or whatever floats your boat. Let go, and pretend you can easily afford everything there. Just live in the affluence. Wear the energy of those around you that swim in money so much that a seven-dollar cup of coffee, or a seventeen-dollar cocktail is nothing.

Remember, any idea about them that isn't loving is yours to 'clean up'. Sometimes when we say the top 1% is doing all these evil things, we are projecting. They are still holy children of God. Remember, what God gives to others, God gives to you. When you come back home, appreciate what you have, really send love to your home and your favorite cup, your socks. Notice what you already have is somehow perfect and might be even more amazing than you previously imagined.

92. BREAK VOWS OF POVERTY

Sometimes we have vows of poverty from a past life. Many women in other points in history, say medieval times, lived in nunneries because it was safe or their husband was killed in one of the many wars. A vow of poverty was sometimes entrance to the nunnery. This shows up in many past life religions, and the idea of it is really spiritual. God is source in all things. Unlimitedness is also of God. Did you make a vow of poverty? You can break it in a holy second – God is my wealth, I now have the perfect amount of money flowing in my life.

Money will show up because you like it. It is okay to have money. Are you careful about how you hold money in your purse or wallet? Is it nicely aligned and treated with love like it's sacred. Handle money with love – what you love is multiplied and amplified. Love money – its okay to love people with money. It is not that money is the root of all evil; it is seeing money as a finite form is the root of all evil. Money is a symbol for the promise (the flow and circulation of energy) behind it. The flow isn't evil. Electricity can be used for good or bad, it can light homes and it can hurt you if you put your finger in a light socket, but the electricity itself is just energy.

Your faith that money is an energy flow, and that the energy is limitless is a part of how we direct the flow of it.

How money is spent determines how much flows: if we are in alignment with Spirit, the flow is unlimited, if we have limiting beliefs, the flow is just as limited. When we pay our bills with the gratitude that services were given us on faith, and wallowing in the good we received, the dress, or the electricity, the food, we increase the flow. When we give to others out of a sense of joy, we increase our havingness, just as giving a healing is receiving a healing, or giving forgiveness is receiving forgiveness.

When we tithe to that which causes our soul to sing, or shine brighter, we are increasing the quality of what is circulating toward us and through us. When we grudgingly pay a bill, curse the envelope, we are asking for that same energy back.

93. GROUND AND GOD

Find that unopened bill you hate to pay, that one you even dread opening the envelope. First ground the envelope. Just give it a separate grounding cord, and ground off all the energy, good or bad, ground off until the bill is neutral. Don't open it yet.

How to Ground

Grounding is energy. It is a beam of light, a tube, and idea that connects what is grounded to the center of the earth. The center of the earth recycles energy and will take any vibration of energy you want to give it. Just postulate that gravity is strong in your grounding cord. It will take heavy energy; you don't need to know what the energy is. Just know that the grounding takes away anything that isn't working for you. It keeps what you want, and takes pain, unease, fear, sickness, a toothache, lack, guilt, energy causing a headache, anything. You can let go and allow ideas, or even pain to go right down your grounding cord. As a spirit in a body, we are not responsible, when we think we are responsible we take on the energy patterns of problems from those around us, and then get sick or feel pain. In fact the spirit needs to be reminded that it is much more than a body and its job is to rest in God and let the Higher Spirit shine Life, love and Peace through us. When we do that we remind others to do the same- there are no problems at all for Spirits in bodies. Grounding is a way to release energy we mistakenly took on. We are beings of light, and everything is already working. When we perceive problems, we often become responsible for them. This is funny. When we are grounded we are reminded that God doeth the works and our job is to stay amused and enthused.

Things or situations do not move you if you are grounded. People can't push you around when you are grounded. You can ground things or ideas or mental image pictures. You can ground your car, your drive, you home, any unease, your bed, and your 6th chakra. Often we ground our first chakra. This keeps our body effortlessly grounded. You want to have an awareness of your Higher Self present after you ground your body. You don't want to ground your ego, and then forget about your Self. Your Self grounds into God in your heart. Don't think about this, just remember. Your Divine Holy Perfect Spirit animates you. Sense her light and the way she radiantly sparkles in you. Turn up her light until light fills the room you are in. Notice how fun this is! Okay, adjust the light to what feels wonderful.

A beam of light to the center of the planet is easy and effortless. Create a beam of blue light to the center of the earth.

Back to the bill you don't want to pay. Ground the bill. Shake off all the energy. Sense gravity taking all your ideas about abundance that aren't loving as you release the energy of the bill down the grounding cord. Gravity does the work. Your job is to release and let go of energy and limits.

Then connect the envelope to God. Just assign a bright happy light that you will call God. You are postulating-Postulating means, that on some level it is done and it will show up in time. You are just sending an energy template to God. This means, this or better. You let go of it and allow God to do *His Thing.* You are just filling the grounded envelope with the brightest, most loving energy you can imagine. God takes the last step. You may feel the light getting brighter, or a shift – you don't need to. Just allowing the presence of God to go into every single interaction in that bill. Hand the envelope energetically to God.

Then open it. You will notice certain lightness. Notice how you are no longer creating more lack by your thoughts. Pay the bill by sending gratitude to the company. When you finish paying, you can connect the envelope to God, and ask that whatever amount you paid, may they receive 10 times more. May the universe shower them with good!

94. SPIRITUAL GIVING

When we give even 10% to those things that feed our spirit, and inspire us; this tells the universe we want more LIFE. More joy. Remember, you can have all the money in the world, but if it causes you anxiety, to do things that cause pain, causes health issues, then the energy behind the money is working against you, and it becomes the circulation of guilt.

Matthew 16:26

For what will it profit a man if he gains the whole world

and forfeits his soul? Or what shall a man give in return
for his soul?

Gain the world and lose your soul – why do you think this
concept has stayed with us for thousands of years. It is
true and a Divine Law. When you have your soul intact,
are guided by your inner self, you are in the flow, joyful,
share good with others, you are WELLthy. The energy of
your soul, the abundance of God is the same as the flow
of money, the flow of chi.. It attracts your good to you,
and things, situations, people, communities, work shows
up that is yours to do. If you are a giver in joy, God will
always take care of you. If you are a giver in lack, begin
to notice.

To those who have, Give all to all – a mental law, your
hands will never be empty – you are a dispenser of divine
gifts. When you dwell in giving from a state of joy, you
are making a declaration that you already have! Repeat.
When you give in joy, you are telling all of creation, I
have! When you give grudgingly, you demonstrate, you
don't have enough and it is taken away from what you
have.

Matthew 13:12

Whoever has will be given more, and they will have
abundance. Whoever does not have, even what they have
will be taken from them.

Money becomes symbolic for spiritual awareness and power. Forgiveness, true forgiveness is a declaration that someone never hurt you because you are a holy Child of God and so is the other person. If you are a holy Child of God you are made of what God is. Can God be hurt? Ever? God defines who you are, not the other person or the incident, and this awareness gives you the place to rest your mind. Because you are so WELLthy that you are sitting in grace and see them as God might, as a worthy and holy child of God, and because they are perfect children of God, they could never have sinned. You make a declaration of your perfection and wholeness when you truly forgive – you are telling the other person, for a while, I thought I could be hurt by you but I was mistaken. You cannot diminish me in any way! I am as God created me, I never gave you power to create me to tell me who I am. I am all in all, and I can share this all in all with you by extending love.

Do you see how pure forgiveness is like the circulation of money? You are in no way allowing the outer symptoms of lack to define your inner wealth or how you experience your existence. You are declaring your unlimited wealth by overflowing joy no matter what is happening. You are demonstrating grace and wealth by reminding the greedy corporations that they are not a greedy corporation, they are holy children of God, and you are Soooooo abundant that you are going to wish them the whole kingdom of good and 10 times their money back. And you follow that demonstration to its end. That 10 times money will go to them. It is already done on an energy level, and it will show up in time, perfectly. God doeth the Works. This is true wealth. This is demonstrating an awareness of abundance.

Their bills do not guilt you out; the bills are a wonderful opportunity to demonstrate that no one is in charge of your abundance but God. No one gets to define how much good you can experience, joy, love, and you are so WELLthy, you can share it!

95. EXPIERENCE PURE JOY

Go inside your heart, and experience pure peace,

Experience pure joy,

Experience unlimited release.

Release your peace and joy to all of existence. Notice how you feel, notice how you have more when you give your spiritual gifts.

96. FUN FUND

Give to yourself not things, but appreciation of the love and joy you already have, train your mind to remember that you already have. Notice what you have and lay into that gratitude. List 10 things you are being grateful for, like air, for your body, for your eyelashes, for the people in your life who give you an opportunity to learn.

When you live in the atmosphere of abundance, and do not give into temptation to think about all the things that are not working, you are on an abundant trajectory, stay there, no matter how long it takes, just be in the gratitude.

When you scrimp and save only for emergencies, and do not spend money on things that bring you joy, the universe will bring you emergencies. It is important to spend your money on things that give you joy! That is your life's work.

Have a fun fund. If you can save for emergencies, then you can put even a nickel a week to fun. (You will feel so abundant that a dollar a week for fun is nothing, or ten dollars a week, or fifty.) Use money for fun things or things that feed your inner spirit. Church, travel, singing lessons, dance, exercise, hiking gear or sports equipment, a new journal, music, expression of some sort, _____fill in the blank with whatever it is that floats your boat. Get used to ever-increasing amounts of fun and feeding your soul activities.

Pay yourself first and have having, which radiates more. Paying yourself the first 10% is a self worth law. This is

the same as giving yourself 10 minutes of meditation.
You are telling the whole of creation what is your
priority. When you feed your soul first, declare your
wonderful day, and are grateful for so many things, first
thing in the morning, you are re-ordering what your day
is. When you think you are going to have a tough day
because of things, finite things, this is the best time to
declare to the universe, I am going to have a wonderful
day, no matter what things happen today, I am going to
have a wonderful day. Something wonderful is going to
happen! You can decide to experience joy no matter what
is happening!

Invest in the world we want to live in. Put your IRA or
401 in socially responsible funds. You will feel good
about yourself! Get your money doing things that make
you a good citizen of the world. Donate to the Sierra Club
or some other organization that cares about our earth.

97. HARMONIOUS MONEY

Bringing your money in harmony with your spiritual
values, tithing, paying yourself first, paying your bills
with gratitude to all the people who contributed to the
thing or service you received; you can really lie into the

gratitude and it will change your existence for the better. There are many opportunities for gratitude, for example, Food. There are the seed growers, the farmers, the packers, truckers, and the company chain from growers to store – there are so many people to thank. Then there is the company that made the plate you eat off of, and all the workers there. There is so much harmony, so many people who are giving to your good! Thank them! There is no time or space as spirit, your declaration is good and will help others at the perfect time and place.

The Course in Miracles says that, "The holiest place in heaven is where an ancient sin has been forgiven.....here all of heaven lights up because it is known that what you thought you feared *you loved the most.*" What am I to forgive or let go of? Letting go of condemnation is the first step is allowing God to *give for you.*

98. RELATIONSHIP WITH ALL THAT IS

"Bow down thyself to me and thou shalt come even to me. Take sanctuary with me alone and I shall liberate thee from all sin, by the resplendent Lamp of Wisdom" ~ *Vedic Hymn*

Do you have a question? An issue?

The space between you and your answer is time.

In a miracle, time collapses. Information is simultaneous.

"Miracles are both beginnings and endings. They thus alter the temporal order. They are always affirmations of rebirth, which seem to go back, but really go forward. They undo the past in the present, and thus release the future." ~ A Course in Miracles

There is not one moment when you didn't matter to the whole. You matter. Your presence is needed. God and all creation is lonely without you. You are always being answered.

When you already think you know as an ego, the whole universe is closed off. When you can say to your Spirit, maybe there is something vastly more intelligent than me, your mind opens and wisdom of an all-knowing nature may become now in your awareness. This is pretty much the anatomy of a miracle. When, if even for a holy second, you let go of the limiting ego, the small self, Your True Self can occupy your mind. Ego is your small mind. It is the mind that thinks the physical is all there is. It's the part of us that is chasing effects, it's out there, a new partner, a new car, a new job, new clothes, and it wants things to go a certain way. Happiness depends on things going in a pre-described fashion. Humility is letting the ego disappear and allowing a listening a deep stillness to operate through your intuitional system- this is your higher self and it is the mind of God, it knows when you were born, all your past lives, your future lives, when you will awaken, all your miracle moments, and how to bring harmony into your life.

Yielding utterly to the Divine, yielding our heart, soul, mind, hands, feet—all yield to the Divine and Its Laws, we become Cathedrals; our body and mind are the architecture and Spirit, Its Grace illuminate us. The more meek and surrendering we become the more Divine Light radiates.

Try this. Be in Divine Presence.

I let go of every problem as a problem. I receive every answer as fulfillment

99. HEAR YOUR SONG

Allow Your Higher Self to sing to you now. Listen. Be still and listen. The sweet nectar of the universal love can flow through your systems and heal them, or to say what healing is, to make you aware of your TRUE SELF, which is perfect, never sinned, never broke, never cried, never forgave because it never condemned. Your True Self is the one God created, and it is as perfect as God is. Self love!

Hear your song.

100. CHOOSE AGAIN

You see yourself in your relationships. Who ever you are in a relationship with is always a mirror of one of your many facets. What shows up in your life is an aspect of who you are. So your self-love is always the greatest factor in what shows up in your life. If you want your relationships to improve, realize in any unloving moment that you can choose again with God. You cannot change anything that you are a victim of. They did it to you, therefore they are your God, or greater than God. If you can see, own up to the world being your projection for one holy second, you have the power to change it. If you see the world as projecting on you, you have no power to change it. So, here is one way of arriving at this Universal law of relationships:

John said something that made me angry. I am angry. This doesn't feel good. Hmm I must be in some sort of pain. I must have, (on some subtle level which I am not aware of) chosen to be in pain. Hmmm. It could not have happened unless I participated in the decision. I can laugh at myself because this is an earth school, and I am here to learn. If I am in pain, I have chosen wrongly. God only wills joy, and the Kingdom for me, (so I must have chosen without God).

I can choose again. I can choose to love myself. I can choose to ask God to show me His love now. I can receive Gods love in any moment I want. Grace is the presence of love in the midst of pain and fear. I can nourish by self-love and that is connection to my true Self, which is God. I can choose. I am always choosing. It is not that person out there that is doing it to me, in some subtle way, I chose not to love myself.

I can choose God. I am entitled to miracles. I give up wanting to be right; I want to be happy instead.

Choosing again is always an option. Letting go, connecting with the God of your Heart for one holy second has the power to bring the awareness of God into any situation. God's Laws reverse our everyday body on earth laws.

When your first relationship is with God, with Source, with the Universal Presence of love, people will come into your life as guides, as earth angels, as teachers, and as lovers and partners. You will see that that person that screamed cusswords a minute ago is Jesus himself, coming in one of his many disguises. All people in your life are God showing up. All people in your life are Christ saying, Greater Works than these Ye Shall Do! When you reframe relationships to holy ones, the very reframing changes the outcome.

Hello Quantum Mechanics! Hello $E = mc^2$. We have

power beyond belief that works in the now. NOW. It works by being present to the fact that every problem in your life is here for you to transform you in some way, into a higher state of being. There are no mistakes, no accidents. When trouble happens, you are here to reframe it, to be mobile, to demonstrate Spiritual Magnificence.

Every encounter is a Holy Encounter. ~ A Course in Miracles

If someone is picking a fight with you, dumping their venom on you, declare God is my support. There are no mistakes and no misunderstandings. All mistakes, all misunderstandings are not God, they are unreal and they now vanish into the nothingness from which they came. God is my defense, God is my support! Love is the only power in the universe and there is no other force. There is no opposing force to God. There is no sin, sickness or death. They are not real. Only life is real. Only Love is real. Put your mind in God, not in the problem. Even if chaos is still spewing venom, keep your mind to God. Turn to Love. Turn to Truth.

101. REFRAME YOUR VISION

The outer system of support that you receive is part of an equation of Self Love. Faith builds the bridge one problem at a time when seen correctly as love in disguise. All those times when you had a problem, but had faith that a loving outcome was assured and it was, create a firm foundation of faith. It starts with you. When you revision any situation as a learning situation, you re-frame the issue and take a step back. The overall, bigger picture is available when you reframe situations. A backward glance that every problem you've ever encountered took you to a place of higher awareness, a higher knowing, we do not blame our mistakes. There are no mistakes; there is only learning and knowledge. Therefore, there are no sinners, no evil, no mistakes, there is only learning. When you take this equation to its future state, or take time out of the equation, we are Spiritually speaking all the highest and most evolved versions of ourselves, because we will all evolve to our highest at some point in the future, when all learning is achieved. There is no time as spirit, so we are already our highest evolved selves, and *we have access to our wise self now by listening to the wisdom of the heart.*

102. HEART ENERGY!

There are research centers now that measure the heart energy, and they conclude the energy of the heart is 1000 times more than energy field of the brain. We have all sorts of currents, and fields of energy, and science is just beginning to prove heart power and the laws of the heart space. You don't need science to tell you what you already know when you listen to your Divine Self.

You are always in charge, you decide how to see who you are in any situation. The more resistant you are, time stretches, the less resistant, time collapses. This is an unusual concept that the Course in Miracles explains. What this means is that the learning that would take thousands of years if you did not listen to spirit, is learned in one holy second if you become available to hearing, knowing God within and willing to act on that knowledge. You collapse lessons in time because they are learned, known, shared. Your life demonstrates this knowledge when coincidences show up, or demonstrations.

103. PRINCIPLES OF MIRACLES

Here are a few **PRINCIPLES OF MIRACLES from A Course in Miracles:**

1.   There is no order of difficulty among miracles. One is not "harder" or "bigger" than another.

They are all the same. All expressions of love
are maximal.

2.   Miracles as such do not matter. The only thing
     that matters is their Source, Which is far beyond
     human evaluation.

3. Miracles occur naturally as expressions of love.
    The real miracle is the love that inspires them. In
    this sense, everything that comes from love is a
    miracle.

5.   All miracles mean life, and God is the Giver of
     life. His Voice will direct you very specifically.
     You will be told all you need to know.

104. BREATHING SPIRIT

Do Nothing. Be still. Be so still the only awareness is of
your breath. Feel air go past your ribs down to your
stomach. Feel your stomach push the air out. Feel the
chambers in your back fill up. Your whole back can
absorb air. Take a breath that expands your lungs 20
percent more than you ever have before. Feel the ribcage
unlock, feel your ribs expand, push them. Our lungs are

huge and can expand more and more with each breath.

Exhale it all out. Keep pushing to zero. Hold it.

Breathe in the Holy Spirit as you breath in all the way to your toes. As you exhale, say, I am under no laws but Gods.

105. BODY LOVE

Are you feeling any tense areas? On your next exhale bring the energy of your breath to this area. Send gratitude to your body. Thank you toes, your legs, your organs, your shoulders, and all the places inbetween. Send love to your body meditation. Thank the air, thank head, and brain, thank thankfullness.

106. LIFE LOVE

THINK OF Ten things that are working well now.

List them.

Savor them.

Self love is love in our relationships. Our first relationship is with God. The universe. When we do this God shows up in our relationships. When you put your first thought on God within, you create miracles in your life. The Universe speaks to you when you say hello to it. Practice that this week. Say hello to the universe and listen. It's just like the money concept. Your attention is creating what shows up in your life. If you attention is on the outer, you create limit. When your attention is on God, God shows up in people, in abundance, in loving moments, in your Beingness. You become aware of the miracle in people and they are gifts brought to you by a loving Universe that is conspiring at all times for your joy.

God is the Light in which I see.
God is the mind with which I think.
God is the Love in which I forgive.
God is the strength in which I trust.

107. INTUITION

All people are intuitive. Awareness first takes faith. In the end, we know what is working by how we feel. This is how all inner practices should be judged: Do I feel a deep peace, which cannot be disturbed? If not, then whatever I did, that color, that vibration represents something that doesn't bring peace, if I see it again, I will know it is an illusion and I will take it out at its root and return it to the nothingness from which it came! (Only God is real) I will turn to the vibration of love and bask in it and then allow a more loving approach to present itself.

Ernest Holmes says: "The powers which are exhibited through the psychic life do really exist in man, and someday he will make conscious use of them and will, thereby be greatly benefited."

Psyche means soul; psychic phenomena are the phenomena of the soul. There are levels of inner awareness. We have an ego inner self who creates on a level of lack and a Spiritual inner awareness, which creates from abundance.

I can say to just about anyone, except a skeptic who is a person inclined to question or doubt all accepted opinions, so someone who is in doubt will not see a thing because their doubt overrides Spirit by their God given intention. If someone doesn't want to have an open mind, they will not see, and they chose that. Faith and imagination are of God and work best by invitation. We have to invite. Faith works. If you have faith that you have inner sight, you will. Making a declaration that you have no inner sight will create just that. That is faith working to close your inner sight. So declare your inner sight is divinely opening perfectly under grace.

Imagine a rose, see the rose, what color is it, what does it smell like. You can imagine a rose, you will smell something with you inner capacities. Allow it to disappear.

Imagine another rose and have this rose represent your challenges, and that rose might look a little different than the first rose. This is pretty easy to do. What ever you see is what you see. But, why in the world would you want to spend your time looking at challenges when you can look at Life? If we look at a rose for God, there needs to be some stillness in the mind, silence, space, something unlimited so the unlimited can speak its language. There are no rules for this except surrender and humility. There is a different seeing for the Universal. In the first and second rose we are seeing our ego self and its projections, it is unique. In the God rose, it is a Universal. It is not unique; it is shared with all humanity. We are at once transformed. We may not see a thing, but we will know its effects. In my inner sanctuary, God is known, but not seen directly. I can know what a rose looks like with divine qualities and what a rose looks like that is an effect. It has certain qualities. Okay. Quit looking at roses and overflow with Divine Love. My cup runneth over!

After any playing with interior mental images, complete with an overflowing awareness of God, so you are left without any residual effect of images or programming. Sense Divine Love as real and undoing anything which is not God's Loving Will. If it's not God it isn't real. Or Thy Will be Done!

108. YES SELF

Notice your Joy of Beingness. Tune into your Beingness. Thank Good for your Joy of Beingness. Notice what you are grateful for increases. Notice that you have more Joy of being. Thank Good for your Life. Thank Good or God for your Strength.

We are going to become friends with our Higher Self, our Yes Self and use her to demonstrate. Your Higher Spirit is the Holy Spirit, and knows Good, your Krishna Self, or Buddha Self.. which is in everyone! It might feel like pure inspiration, or a Rejoicing. You have your own way of Being in this Consciousness. Give yourself permission.

Sometimes an invitation is needed to open the heart door. Open all doors in your Mind to your Higher Self, who is always whispering great news in your inner ear. Can you take a moment to listen? Write down this inspiration:

109. GLORY SELF

Get quiet, and listen to your Higher Self. What fabulous thing is she telling you? Ask her for a demonstration of Good. She is an aspect of God, the translator, so this is really all she lives for. She knows your reason for being here and guides you on how you can transform problems into spiritual magnificence. The root word of Human being means dispenser of divine Gifts. Get a sense of what this means for you. Arise! She is a sense of Glory, and you have to awaken your consciousness so you can hear her and know her. Awaken this aspect of yourself. What Divine Gifts is your Higher Self willing you now?

Listen with your inner ears.

Draw or write what you see.:

Sense your gratitude for this Spiritual communication. When you receive communication like this feel your gratitude and agreement. Each time you do this you make it easier to hear and know the next time. Each time you capture this information you make the next time easier. Even if the message makes no sense, or it is in a vibration or a color, make an entry in your journal. You are making the next time easier by acting on it. Each time you act on this information you bring more of this knowledge forward. **Where your joy is your treasure is.** This information is always joyful, it is abundant to hear guidance. You get a sense of her in your deepest quietest moments so you can use her when chaos, upset strikes.

110. MOVE YOUR MOUNTAIN!

…or play with it…

Next time you are stuck in traffic, or some other stuck situation, and really defeated and have anger or feel victimized by the hours stuck. Take a breath, a deep breath and instead of reacting, summon and have a conversation with your Higher Self. Tell her your situation, and what would be your greatest joy in this moment, what is your answered prayer?

Really relax into this.. you have time, your stuck in traffic.

Listen carefully and know a joyful answer is coming in some way. Maybe in a traffic jam the answered prayer would be flow.

If your answered prayer was something like flow, Inwardly, Shout your Yesssss that there is great flow, do not stop, and praise God that there is flow, that everyone in the stuck traffic is dispensing their Divine Gifts of divine movement. Imagine, get animated, and sing! Some **Great strength of you and in you is only born in the midst of lack.** It's the faith in and of your strength that's really born.

Keep faith even if nothing moves. Train your mind to rejoice and celebrate and to keep enthused no matter what! Notice I'm not saying shut your eyes to the facts; be aware of traffic conditions, just refuse to allow the traffic to disappoint you or defeat you.

Rejoice. Laugh, sing, dance, and know that wherever you are, All the power of Heaven and earth of God is there too. Let it out! Sing your good! You have an inner voice that can shout hallelujah good at the top of your inner lungs! Blast your inner good! All of God, the whole universe is conspiring for your good. Hallelujah! Every person in the traffic is a holy child of God, who would really like to sing with you. Sense their songs of joy, that their soul is always singing.

Get a sense of moving the stuck energy with your enthusiasm, you are not using your own energy. You are channeling Divine energy. It is love and cannot harm. If you feel you are channeling anger you will only increase the stuckness.

The traffic will move or not, but better, you moved your personal energy and created light in the midst of darkness and anger. You begin to use problems as opportunities to try out and hone your tools. See what works for you. You will find the inner chord and how you strike it and change happens.

The truth of any matter is that wherever there is a problem; right beside it You, the Dispenser of Divine Gifts is also there with a perfect answer. The problem and its solution are born in the same moment. You have, at any time, a choice to dwell in a problem or its solution. You always have a choice. You can choose to dwell in the solution, even though you don't yet know what it is.

Loud, active, rebellious, unleashed faith in the face of problems upgrades things in other areas of your life as well as the situations you are presently in. You may be guided to drive with an added guidance that helps you and others. Be open to seeing how this changes things in areas that seem unrelated.

Later, write the good that happened. (Only the positive.)

111. WAKE UP

"Awake up, my glory!" Ps. 57:8
"Awake thou that sleepest!" Eph 5:14
"Rise up my Soul!" Emma Curtis Hopkins

The bible is a book, that you can take or leave, but when you decide to see it as part of yourself, that there are symbols, and metaphors that represent the inner workings of our own consciousness, the bible becomes an alchemy cookbook. When we see the story of Christ, from sacred birth, to teaching and healing, to suffering on the cross and then to transcending the world and becoming a living eternal being, we can be talking about our own conscious progression as we go through problems or situations to solutions.

That the story of Christ is repeated in ancient Egyptian texts with Horus, the same elements- the stars, the virgin, the rebirth and this same story is the story of Buddha and Krishna and many other sages, there is either ancient telephone tag going on, or there are symbols behind the elements in these myths from the bible, the Koran, Buddhism, that are common to all minds. The symbols of betrayal, of healing, of transcending we all go through.

That is why these stories, myths, metaphors behind the words survive to this day. There is truth, which awakens the finer aspects of our minds if we view the stories as symbolic.

When the king of the Gods told Gautama (who became Buddha) while he sat under the banyan tree that he was to teach, to remember that all of us are teaching all the time, and to consider what we are teaching.

If you look at consciousness as a vertical scale, much like the havingness gauge, we can choose to stay horizontal, and live in a certain vibration, even if it brings us pain, or we can choose to rise up the scale, much like the emotional scale, from disappointment at the bottom, up to curious, happy, enthusiasm, joy – knowing we can go up that scale any time we want and intention starts the action – even if you don't feel a certain way, you have the option to laugh, and get out of the cycle, remember, an inward, ha, ha, ha even if said pathetically, is funny. If you keep repeating ha, ha ha, even screaming it, it will change things, you have stepped out of the situation and now, for a split second you have a choice, to remember, alone, you are powerless over the situation, but you walk with a power greater than you, and it is inside you this very moment. It may not enter your field of consciousness without invitation. You step out of the situation and remember Love. Remember, grace is the presence of love in a world of seeming hatred and pain.

And you invite grace, Yes, God, now God. Thank you for stepping in now Holy Spirit. Good will happen.

Choice is your power.

It takes one holy second when all the laws of this world are reversed. One second, remember who you are.

Knowing that God is your stillness, and silence. It's always there. You can always take a look-see and notice what chakra someone is in. This is a spiritual hello to them. It makes them aware that they are a spirit in a body. You can do this silently, and they may ever know consciously what happened, but you do. You don't need to talk to them. Just inwardly smile and go on your way. This looking at chakra's changes when we consider the I AM prayer:

I Am The Soul

I AM that I AM.

I AM not the body.

I AM not the emotions.

I AM not the thoughts.

I AM not the mind.

The mind is only

A subtle instrument of the soul.

I AM the Soul.

I AM a Spiritual being of Divine Intelligence,

Divine Love, Divine Power.

I AM one with the Higher Soul

I AM that I AM.

I AM one with the Divine Spark.

I AM a Child of God.

I AM connected with God.

I AM one with God.

I AM one with ALL.

112. CHRIST WITHIN

Create your Christ light in yourself. (See yourself as the purest, diamond quality light, and pure light. Say hello to the Christ within, see yourself as angelic. I know, we are making this up. The imagination is a god given holy place and God takes the last step- you are showing the universe what you want to show up.)

And go on with your day. This is really healing to those around us, and therefore us, because we are one being.

113. EVERY ENCOUNTER IS A HOLY ENCOUNTER

Every encounter is a holy encounter. Every person is God showing up. Every problem is yours to declare unreal and an opportunity to for you to dwell in Truth. Every person deserves a second chance. Every person deserves to be seen truly. What shows up in our life is ours to transform.

114. FULLFILLMENT USING SIRITUAL LAW

Harmony is.. do no mental work. Don't force thoughts. Allow harmony to reveal its Self.

The God that cannot be named cannot be the infinite God.
~ Lao-tsu

The God that is realized is nameless. In our realization of our oneness with infinite Principle, Love, God, we find and manifest our oneness with every idea necessary to the unfoldment of our completeness.

I am grateful to Ernest Holms for the following affirmative prayer which I've adapted:

As Spirit,

I know there is an inner Spiritual Presence in everything. I know that this Spiritual Presence responds to me. I know that everyone is an incarnation of God, that the living Spirit breathes through all. I recognize this Spirit and It responds to me. I realize that everything is alive, awake and aware with Spirit.

I commune with this Divine Presence. The Spirit within me reaches out and communes with the Spirit in everything and everyone I contact. It is the same Spirit in all, overall and through all.

I have a deep realization that as Spirit, I am surrounded by an infinite Spiritual Law, which receives the impress of my thought and acts creatively upon it. I am conscious of my ability to use Spiritual Law, to direct it for specific purposes, for myself and others. There is nothing in me that can deny, limit, obstruct, divert or in any way hinder my use of Spiritual Law. It is within my own mind, because God is right where I am.

In calm confidence, in perfect trust, in abiding faith and with complete peace, I let go of every problem as a problem. I receive the answer as fulfillment.

Amen.

115. VBCS IS SPIRITUAL LAW

By now you should have the awareness that the VBCS is another way of changing your awareness from abiding in the finite natural laws of this world to consciously abiding in unlimited spiritual law. Now that you know this, you will see versions of it everywhere, now that your mind is trained to see it.

Notice the typical order of church service, Welcome to a holy place, Invocation, (invoke a deity), The message, (wisdom) Thanksgiving (giving thanks creates more), Benediction (devout or formal invocation of blessedness).

An affirmative prayer,

God is

I am

I know

I am grateful

I release and let it go

the Lords Prayer,

Our father who art in heaven

Give us our supply

this Psalm. You will see it everywhere.

The method is for all to use.

Aramaic Version of the Lords Prayer

O, Birther of the Cosmos, focus your light within us --
make it useful
Create your reign of unity now
Your one desire then acts with ours,
As in all light,
So in all forms,
Grant us what we need each day in bread and insight:
Loose the cords of mistakes binding us,
As we release the strands we hold of other's guilt.
Don't let surface things delude us,
But free us from what holds us back.
From you is born all ruling will,
The power and the life to do,
The song that beautifies all,
From age to age it renews.
I affirm this with my whole being.

116. PSALM 23

23 The Lord is my shepherd; I shall not want.

² He maketh me to lie down in green pastures: he leadeth me beside the still waters.

³ He restoreth my soul: he leadeth me in the paths of righteousness for his name's sake.

⁴ Yea, though I walk through the valley of the shadow of death, I will fear no evil: for thou art with me; thy rod and thy staff they comfort me.

⁵ Thou preparest a table before me in the presence of mine enemies: thou anointest my head with oil; my cup runneth over.

⁶ Surely goodness and mercy shall follow me all the days of my life: and I will dwell in the house of the Lord for ever.

This scripture commands the Lord to still us. He leads me to still waters, he restoreth my soul (even though it may be scarlet with sin).

Can you feel the restoration and the presence. It is done in this psalm! Even though I walk in the shadow of broken dreams, joy killers, enslaving personalities, death, I shall not fear (the world of form) Spiritually, Thou art with me. Thy rod and staff they comfort me.. there is spiritual learning. And with Spiritual learning and principle, Thou annointest my head, and preparest a feast before my enemies! Isn't that a good one!! Surely goodness and mercy shall follow me all the days of my life-- because by now in the scripture you are already dwelling in God. And I shall dwell in the house of the lord forever.

If you've ever had one moment of awareness of God making your way easier, or healing you or showing you love instead of fear, just one moment.. do you think God will withhold that from you again? Ever.. if you've ever been touched by spirit, it is with you forever. This awareness is eternal and you build on it every time you remember it.

117.ASTRAL BODY

At night, before you go to sleep, remember all the good things that happened to you today, and all the miracles. Give thanks for your life and all the people in it. Thank your bed, thank your astral body. You may want to pack the room with angels, or bring your room to light, divine heavenly light. Thank the light. The light has life and intelligence. It likes to be seen and acknowledged and it will increase if you thank it.

118. GROUND

When we ground, we are connecting to gravity.

We release excess energy, thoughts, vibrations that we may have collected from the news, or minds that are offering thoughts that are not helpful at this time. Some ideas were helpful thoughts or ideas in the past, but now you've 'been there done that and have moved on', and the ideas are energetic clutter. You can release that energy that keeps that clutter around by grounding. You allow energetic clutter to go down to the center of the earth. You may imaging a beam of light, a giant redwood, a sparkly river of light, a color. Or just do it. Ground. What works one day may not work the next day. Grounding cords can be changed daily. now, just imagine a release to the earth anything that is not serving you. Let it go.

People who are aware of energy are often healers. Healing can mean taking on the problems of others. Women are wired to do this.. ha ha ha it is wired to the genetics of making babies and raising them. A healer may ask, and this is how you know you are a super healer.. is why do I want to mess up the planet by sending my unwanted energy to it's center? At the center of the planet is a great recycling center (magma) and it converts energy to be non-charged. Then energy is free to be used again in a neutral form. What do I mean by charged? Have you ever felt when someone was so mad at you, you could feel their anger? You suddenly felt angry too, or deflated. That is one kind of energy that if you are grounded, it will go right down your grounded and you can remain in your good mood. Sometimes hysteria can feel like a buzzing and you can ground that out as well.

When someone wants to sway you into their way of thinking, if you are ungrounded, that may program you to do things that have nothing to do with your purpose or your path. You can ground a situation. I ground my car, my path and connect the whole thing to God. Then my driving experience is wonderful no matter what's going on.

You can ground your house, your neighbors house, your street. I love to ground my house and connect it to God.

How do you connect something to God? You just do it. It is a personal idea, and God is personal to everyone. God can be wherever or whatever you think It is. Universal Love, or the Supreme Being.. whatever works.

Try it. Ground. Release. What do you notice?

Connect to God. Sit with this..what do you notice?

Ground in God. Just allow yourself to do this, however you do this. Notice.

Spiritual awareness is created by using your energy to do a repeatable activity and then noticing. You don't read about it and then you have it. Reading about push ups is not doing push ups.

It is created, the spiritual relationship is a foundation and from this, you can do all sorts of really fun things!

119. GOD SUNS

Become as a child. Be your kindergarten self. This is a good tool that is foundational just like the grounding cord, but it works best if you are playing and keeping it simple. Also.. some amusement keeps this really fast and simple. Be amused. Can you laugh at yourself? We are being really silly here..

Rub your palms together. This opens your hand chakras. Rub till you feel some heat. hold your hands above your head. Shoulders width up.. Feel a gold sun. A sparkly shining clear golden sun. Some people can feel energetic vibrations. Others are learning. Others don't want to learn. They still have hand chakras. Use it or lose it. Spiritual awareness happens with experience. The more you do it, the more powerful you are. So start with the best!

Create a golden sun. Envision it, imagine it. ..or however you do it..right over your head, and you are holding the sun. we are all different. Image in this, your highest creative essence, your growth vibration, and your present time growth vibration. You Know how to do this.. just do it. Pretend..Maybe if you shut your eyes its easier. sprinkle in amusement. Feel your arms widen as the sun grows larger. Are you too serious? You will learn where serious gets you! This is funny.. you are learning how spirit works.. serious willfulness creates a wall, amusement playfullness creates a way.

Pour this golden sun into your body and shine it out.

Your hand chakras and your upper chakras are joint creators in this. You are using your own energy to create a vibration.

Filling in with a golden sun is a good thing to do after you ground. You just released energy and now you are changing your vibration. Your energy attracts the same vibration unless you change it. You want a higher vibration, that's why you are keeping it playful and amused, which are very high vibrations.

It's fun to play with vibrations, but keep it positive. Imagine Christ energy in your sun. What does that feel like? Imagine the vibration of abundance, does your sun sparkle or go whiter? finer? Clearer?

You can create a golden sun around your body from your heart chakra. This is really fun. From your heart, shine out light. You can shine it around you or you can shine it so much it encircles the whole world. You are just playing with energy. Keep it fun, keep it simple.

Can you notice a radial quality? This is a health vibration. Increase your health vibration to your highest health vibration and have it shine out from within.

Bring your golden sun around your body.

As a child you can play with the idea..be like a kindergarten kid, and just play with this idea…. you were created by the hands of the Supreme Being and have incarnated in many lifetimes. The mind that created the universe shares thoughts with you....and has since the beginning. The ability to create a Spiritual body is within you, the ability to bring forth from your divine template, your eternal youthful strong healthy body is in your knowledge. A Spiritual body is always perfect. It is only our mind which can create anything other than perfections. We can postulate the Divine is doing the Divine work in this to bring forward our perfect health.

120. HEALING

You practice on your own (seeming) problems so you can help others. You see how your practice works on your situations and build it so your faith is so strong it like a lever that moves the world when you called on to heal.

Sometimes sickness is just stubborn stuck energy. You can literally feel the dense stuck energy in your hands if you have a stiff neck, or a foot issue. If a friend has a pain somewhere, ask if you can feel the energy density with your hands. (rub you hands together to open the chakras) and then notice the areas of pain compared to other areas. If you are aware of energy, you can then channel Divine Energy through your hands to the areas of dense energy, or scoop away the dense energy and then replace it with Divine Energy or neutral energy. Don't use your energy, don't put your personal vibration into another body. It's rude and can make them sick. Use Universal Light, Christ Force or Divine which has intelligence to morph into whatever they body system needs. You will know it by how your hand chakras feel. Your hands may even be guided.

You want to be grounded when you do this. You also don't want to channel just because you can. You want energy that feels light and joyful. Putting the wrong gas in the car destroys the car and it's the same with energy into another persons space.

If your hands are aware of energy, it's great to take classes to learn more about this.

You can begin to see how getting in a problem and then getting out of it makes you a better healer. You have your own healing gifts, and here is something to consider if you can feel energy with your hands.

121. HEALING HANDS

This is one of the first foundational classes Divine Healing Centers teach. Everyone is expected to know this practice, and they practice on everyone who walks in the door.

You can open your hand chakras and create your healing hands. This is fun!

1.Thank Spirit for the Perfect Guidance and delivery. You want to have that Divine energy right in your hand chakras. Imagine Divine Light Gloves the size of potholders. Feel it, know it, allow it, be grateful that it's working perfectly, and that you are surrendering your will to the Divine Will. Be Meek. Surrender to the Divine

Light Welling up in you, or wherever it is coming forth.

2.Just postulate that your hands have a bright, sparkling golden energy, or….

3.Run your Divine Energy from your Crown and heart chakras. Or…

4.You can also channel Chi or Prana force from one hand and send it through the other. Or…

5.Another way is to ask an Angel or Healing Master to guide your hands.

6. The point here is that you don't use your own energy, and that you have a prayer before and after the healing to direct how the Divine goes about the healing through you. The Saint Francis Prayer is a good one. For some people they just see the perfect health of the healee, others use their hands, others declare it…we are all on different paths and levels, so tune into what is right for you. You will learn your distinct gifts.

7. Just having an idea that the Divine Will and Source is guiding your in your healing, and turn to that Light.

8. Turn completely to that Divine Light and allow yourself to be a channel for the healing, and then you will say, think, and know how to direct the energy or what to say or use your Mind or the Divine Will in you.

9. With your hands, feel around in front of the chakras noticing any dense or gritty energy.

10. Move your hands around the body and notice the perimeter of that dense energy and begin to move it out. Just scoop it up with your palm and move it completely out of the aura.

11. You may want to shake your hands out afterward, you want that energy to leave your hands and it will. Just don't absorb it. Stay amused— the worse the energy, the **more amused you are.** Tell bad jokes. Laughing Yoga.. (to yourself) Don't match the energy. Match the Divine. Fake amusement works.

12. Chant Ooomm to your hands to reset them, or just know God in your hand chakra's.

13. Create a Sparkling Golden Sun of the healee's Divine Energy, and have the Divine show you how to do this and have it match the healee's highest light. You create it actually in their upper chakras which are already their highest energy, so it's pretty hard to screw up.

14. Liquefy that energy and fill up the body completely so it's glowing with light.

15. Thank Spirit and

16. Ask that a Divine angel of God be assigned to the healee for as long as it takes to see their body and mind into perfect health. Mary, the Mother of Christ is an option if you don't want to deal with angels.

17. Some healing practices add an electric blue around

the chakras or aura to seal in the Divine energy, but you will be guided.

18. Call back any of your energy back in a gold sun above your head. Reset your energy to your highest Creative Essence, your Present Time Growth Vibration and Highest Essence. See yourself overflowing with Radiant Golden Clear Light.

122. CROWN CHAKRA HEALING

So, now that you are aware of this energy inside you, you can move it with your minds eye as well as your hands. You can practice on yourself so then you can to long distance healings. But practice on yourself so you know how easy this is and how your own healing style is. You can't read it in a book, you have to do it to learn it. Practicing you, yourself counts, because then you will have conviction and your faith will be unshakable.

If you ever have a pain, or a toothache, or tightness in your body, become aware of your God energy by getting silent and looking up. You will see a bright light – don't be afraid, you cannot die as a soul, and you are not going through the tunnel. Stop that! The light is always there, it's just maybe you never noticed how close God is. You just look up at your own 7th chakra which is on top of your head and with your mind, grab a ball if this energy and bring it to your tooth or wherever the pain is. Move that bright energy right to the middle of the pain. Of course there is resistance, that is why there's pain. You keep bringing that gold light in no matter what. It might take once, or a day or a week or a year. The key is the attitude of victory- I will have my ease-pain you are the stranger here! If you tell that pain- it will not win and one way or another you are going back into the nothingness you belong to- this attitude will cure just about anything. The reason is- Spirits not only do **not** feel pain, but they are the source of healing. Heal the spirit and the spirit will heal the body. This is not to say don't go to the doctor! Listen! You must go if you feel you need to!

Often medicine does not cure the underlying condition- it masks it with drugs. Worse, drug companies want profit so they are more interested in making you a customer, so you need to take a new drug for the drug that just masked your pain, but now gives you suicidal thoughts. Think about how many people energy healing puts out of work: insurance companies, doctors, nurses, office staff, drug companies, the list goes on.

"Before **you** heal someone, **ask** him **if** he's willing to give up the things that made him **sick**."
            —**Hippocrates**.

No wonder the AMA invalidates all healing methods that don't bring them money. You are the doctor and your intuition is your guide. If you want to use energy here is how to do it. You still have to go to the doctor if you need to, and for this reason, we are grateful to all doctors—they are necessary!!! Still, you can do energy work.

You can use your hands to move the energy or your mind. You can feel this. It's amazing how quickly and boldly it works. You are the Light of the world. If you do no works, you lose consciousness of your abilities and your Light.

The minute you sense this energy wants to darken your day, and have the attitude of, I get to 'play' with it, the game is already won. You are taking command and control and are no longer a victim. You can move the energy out before it takes up residence and becomes a physical ailment. You know what harmony feels like in your body, what ease feels like.

Your 7th chakra has unlimited God energy. It is not depleted by using it. It is good to go up there and hang out when meditating.

Troward points out the holographic quality of God. If you have a spark of God, one little awareness of love, or peace, or any quality of God, then you have ALL OF GOD. At any point, all of creation is there. Let this sink in… because it is yours to use!

So, if you are having a stubborn pain problem, for example with your knees. You can find where you know

God is, and direct that to the knees. Or, just declare, ALL of God is in my knees, and keep flooding the knees with this knowledge. Tell that pain it does not have a chance because the Creator of the Universe that is Omnipresent, Omniscient and Omnipotent is on this in the perfect way. Now the Supreme Creator is restoring the eternal divine blueprint and all the correct information for your eternally youthful strong knees. God is flooding anything connected to the knees with God Force. Keep at it until the energy shifts. Do not go into well I have a torn this and a busted that.. let go of the natural law and dwell in Spiritual Law where all is done in the now. The energy template will be restored if you keep at it. You may be guided to go the doctor, ice it, or take supplements such as gelatin, or rest much longer than you think you need to, or even get it operated on. You have to listen and go to the doctor if this is clear to you.

I thought I had bad knees for years. At the Center for Spiritual Living I took a Roots class about Troward, and I used the information immediately on my knees. What worked was insisting on unlimited God in my knees. Of a sense of Standing in God. When I moved the pain energy out, I found there were race ideas on aging, like at a certain age your knees are supposed to be fragile. This is simply not true. You have embedded information on how to create a body for many lifetimes- hundreds or thousands. If you can keep creating a body every time you are reborn into a new life, then you can create strong knees any time you want. Direct the Spirit and the Spirit will heal the body.

Emma Curtis Hopkins says we are made in the image and likeness of God and God is Spirit. Our Spirit, with the knowledge of God, creates our bodies. You must insist and intend with Faith from God!

WEEKLY REMINDERS

MONDAY

I accept the fullness of My Own Divine Well-Being

"Within myself is that which is perfect, that which is complete, that which is divine; that which was never born and cannot die; that which lives, which is God-the Eternal Reality."

Today I seek to express my Essence in all that I think, say, and do. I let my Holiness shine in my life and world.

TUESDAY

I accept the fullness of My Own Divine Well-Being

"Every image of fear is erased from my mind, every sense of confusion leaves my thought. My mind now entertains and reflects the Divine into everything which I do, say and think-into my body, in my affairs."

Today I express the Holiness of my love for my Self. I let

go of the confusion and the fear that is not founded in my Essence. I now let myself experience being an esteemed Child of God. I express the esteemed Child of God in all that I think, say, and do.

WEDNESDAY
I accept the fullness of My Own Divine Well-Being

"The Divine within me is Wholeness, and my mind reflects this Wholeness into every organ, every function, every action, every reaction of my physical being, renewing it after the Perfect Pattern-the Christ within me."

Today I reflect on that Perfect Christ within me. I let go of all the images that no longer serve that Holy Christ within. I seek the Christ image within myself and all others that I meet in this Spiritual Day.

THURSDAY
I accept the fullness of My Own Divine Well-Being

"Universal Substance reflects Itself, into my mind, into

daily supply, so that everything I need each day is supplied. Before the need, is the thing, and with the apparent need, it is met."

I am open to receiving my Divine Good. I am an esteemed Child of God and an heir to all the Good that God has created for me. I open my heart and my mind to the Good that surrounds me. Today, I look for the Good and praise it.

FRIDAY
I accept the fullness of My Own Divine Well-Being

"There is Something within me which goes before me and prepares the way wherever I go, making straight the way, making perfect the way, making immediate and instant, and permanent and harmonious, every situation."

Faith is my gift. I walk with an increased faith in my Essence and my Holy nature. I know today that my Holy nature goes before me and makes my way clear.

SATURDAY
I accept the fullness of My Own Divine Well-Being

"I am never alone, never lonely, for I have as companions
and friends those people who are drawn to me by the
ever-active and immutable Law of Attraction."

Today I embrace all that I am and focus my energy in
expressing that great Essence of Love that I am. I see the
return of the Love that I am in every situation and person
that I come into contact with. Today is the day that Love
has made.

SUNDAY
I accept the fullness of My Own Divine Well-Being.

"Abundance is mine. I cannot be deprived of my supply.
The trees do not lack for leaves, nor do flowers fail to
bloom. Am I not as important as they?"

The Essence that I am is abundant. I have abundant self-
esteem. I am filled with the greatness of God, and the
Holiness that I am abounds through all my activities.
Today I am committed to an abundant world. I talk, think,
and do only those things that show the abundance of my
true Essence.

Thank you dear reader! Have fun with your new tools!

May God shine on you as you follow your path!

Suggested Inspirational Reading

Spiritual Law in a Natural World, by Emma Curtis Hopkins

How to Use the Science of Mind, by Ernest Holmes.

The Seven Spiritual Laws of Success: A Practical Guide to Fulfillment of Your Dreams, by Deepak Chopra

The Dynamic Laws of Healing, by Catherine Ponder

The Path to Wealth, by May McCarthy

Course in Miracles: Sparkly Edition, by Jesus Of Nazereth

Conversations with God, Neale Donald Walsh

The Complete Works, by Florence Scovel Shinn

The Science of Mind, by Ernest Holmes

Life Visioning, by Michael Bernard Beckwith

ACKNOWLEDGMENTS

Thank you to Spirit! Thank you to my mother and father— I wouldn't be here without them, so THANK YOU! I have unwavering gratitude for my family and friends who continually support me in moments of doubt and joy. I am lucky to have you in my life.

Much gratitude to Deepak Chopra for major inspiration for this book!

I am grateful to all those who have crossed my path in recent years and contributed to my journey of self acceptance. You helped me so much. Thank you to everyone who has read versions of this and helped me along the path. Profound gratitude to all my coaching clients, students who I have been so blessed to have in my life—thank you for your faith and practice. Love and blessings to Connie Portola, Wendy Matthews, Greg Nelson and Mary McCloy for showing me this material is fun and powerful to use in a class setting.

Heart filled Love and blessings to Jeanne Rose, for your presence in my life and for planting the seeds that started this book. I love you.

I must acknowledge the Church of Divine Man's mystical teachings of Christianity. Great thanks to all my spiritual teachers, Karl Vidt and Course in Miracles teachers everywhere and to those with a spiritual practice. Great thanks to Catherine Ponder, Florence Scovel Shin and Emma Curtis Hopkins who's ideas are seeped in these pages. Gratitude for the teachings of Micheal Bernard Beckwith and Louis Bostwick.

Special thanks to Dr. David Bruner, Rev. Susan Overland and Rev. Queen Michel Jordan and the fantastic tribe and choir at the Center for Spiritual Living in San Jose, your songs are singing in this book.

I could not have written this book without my husband, Rob Andrews; you have taught me so much, and your patience and generosity, your goodness and unabashed truth inspires me always.

ABOUT THE AUTHOR

Brooke Scudder Andrews has illustrated over 25 books, and is the author of The Colors of Paris, and Spiritual Power Tools: Dream Fulfillment Toolkit. She was ordained in the Church of Divine Man in 1989. Since then she has continued to learn and study in different spiritual arenas, and teach in various Spiritual Centers. She has a unique perspective of faith with fun.

To learn more to go to www.omgican.com

Made in the USA
Middletown, DE
05 May 2021